BEHIND THE CAMERA

James Cameron

Ron Howard

Spike Lee

George Lucas

Rob Reiner

Steven Spielberg

Steven Spielberg

Elizabeth Sirimarco

Chelsea House Publishers
Philadelphia

Frontis: Spielberg directing *Jurassic Park.*

CHELSEA HOUSE PUBLISHERS

EDITOR IN CHIEF Sally Cheney
DIRECTOR OF PRODUCTION Kim Shinners
CREATIVE MANAGER Takeshi Takahashi
MANUFACTURING MANAGER Diann Grasse

STAFF FOR **STEVEN SPIELBERG**

ASSOCIATE EDITOR Ben Kim
PRODUCTION ASSISTANT Jaimie Winkler
PICTURE RESEARCHER Sarah Bloom
SERIES AND COVER DESIGNER Takeshi Takahashi
LAYOUT 21st Century Publishing and Communications, Inc.

©2002 by Chelsea House Publishers,
a subsidiary of Haights Cross Communications.
All rights reserved. Printed and bound in the United States of America.

http://www.chelseahouse.com

First Printing

1 3 5 7 9 8 6 4 2

Library of Congress Cataloging-in-Publication Data

Sirimarco, Elizabeth, 1966-
    Steven Spielberg / Elizabeth Sirimarco.
        p. cm.—(Behind the camera)
Includes bibliographical references and index.
    ISBN 0-7910-6714-9 (hardcover)
    1. Spielberg, Steven, 1947- —Juvenile literature. 2. Motion picture
producers and directors—United States—Biography—Juvenile literature.
I. Title. II. Series.
PN1998.3.S65 S57 2002
791.43'0233'092—dc21

                                                                2002003771

Table of Contents

Long before directing films like *E.T.* and *Close Encounters of the Third Kind* (seen here), a teenage Steven Spielberg already had his head in the stars. At 17, Spielberg directed the alien visitation film *Firelight,* using an 8mm camera and a budget of $600.

Chapter 1

"I'm Going to Make Movies"

ON MARCH 24, 1964, a searchlight crossed the night sky of Phoenix, Arizona. Something exciting was happening, and people all over Phoenix had heard about the event. "Firelights Capture Earthlings in Film Premiering Tuesday," announced a headline in the *Arizona Republic.* Posters, billboards, and radio stations told of a movie premiere that would take place at the Phoenix Little Theater. This was no ordinary movie. It was the first feature-length work of a local filmmaker. And that filmmaker was 17-year-old Steven Spielberg.

During his junior year in high school, Steven had spent his

free time making *Firelight.* He had convinced friends and classmates to give up their weekends and take part in his production. His father had agreed to loan him money for film, props, and other expenses. By that time, Steven Spielberg already had become something of a local celebrity. A few years before, the television news had covered the making of his 40-minute tale of World War II, *Escape to Nowhere,* which he completed in 1962 at the age of fifteen. It won first prize in a statewide amateur film contest, in part because of the realistic special effects the young filmmaker had devised. Later, the *Arizona Republic* ran two articles about the making of *Firelight,* with photo spreads featuring the cast and crew. Although he was only seventeen, the people of Phoenix had already taken notice of Steven Spielberg. Could they expect great things from him in the future?

It is often said that a key to happiness is doing what you love, but not everyone is lucky enough to turn a favorite activity into a full-time job. And those who are will tell you that there is a price—hard work and dedication. Steven Spielberg is one person who is lucky enough—and committed enough—to spend his life doing what he loves most: making movies. The more time he spent behind the camera, the more he knew he wanted to be a director when he grew up. After the premiere of *Firelight,* Steven told reporters that making movies "grows on you. You can't shake it. . . . I want to write movie scripts, but I like directing above all. All I know for sure is I've gone too far to back out now."

Firelight tells the story of mysterious aliens who travel to Earth, plotting to abduct Earthlings for an extraterrestrial zoo. Although it cost only about $600 to make, the movie features special effects that amazed his audience on that day back in 1964. How could a teenager, with his father's 8mm movie camera, make a film that rivaled Hollywood science-fiction flicks of the day? (The width of film is given in millimeters, and the wider the film, the better the picture. Professional films are shot on 35mm film.) Steven's fascination with special effects and science fiction continued to flourish, inspiring some of the movies for which he is most famous. *Firelight* is a forerunner of the multimillion-dollar spectaculars that Steven has made as an adult, a preview of coming attractions.

A special memory inspired Steven to write the story for *Firelight*. "One night my dad woke me up in the middle of the night and rushed me into our car in my night clothes," he remembers. Ten-year-old Steven did not know what was happening, and he was a little bit frightened. They drove for about half an hour before Arnold Spielberg stopped the car. They got out, and Arnold pointed to the sky. "There was a magnificent meteor shower," recalls Steven. "All these incredible points of light were crisscrossing the sky." Arnold and Steven spread out a blanket, lay down, and looked up at the heavens in wonder.

That night in the Arizona desert inspired more than *Firelight*. Some twenty years later, Steven made a "remake" of that film, a movie he called *Close Encounters of the Third Kind*. In that 1977 science-fiction classic, actor Richard Dreyfuss takes his family out to the country, where they watch by the side of the road as mysterious and beautiful lights dance across the night sky. Today, Steven often uses his childhood experience in his movies. In fact, he once said that he "can always trace a movie idea back to my childhood." By making films, he has found a way to share his thoughts, dreams, fears, and fantasies with millions of people all over the world.

Between 1881 and 1914, two million Jews fled Russia and Eastern Europe for the United States. All four of Steven's grandparents were among these immigrants, searching for a better life in the New World. They settled in Ohio, where both of Steven's parents were born. Steven, too, was born there on December 18, 1946, at Cincinnati's Jewish Hospital. (Many sources say that the year was 1947, but his birth certificate records it as one year earlier.) The family settled in a Jewish suburb of Cincinnati called Avondale. Both sets of grandparents lived nearby.

Right away, people recognized that Steven was special—and maybe a little bit naughty. Steven's mother, Leah, jokes, "When he was growing up, I didn't know he was a genius. . . . My mother used to say, 'The world is going to hear of this boy.' I used to think she said it so I wouldn't kill him." One next-door neighbor described the young man in a single word: "Different." Another used the Yiddish word for crazy: *meshuggeneh*. Steven's father characterizes him as curious and energetic, a boy who was always asking questions.

Steven and his family did not stay long in Avondale. His father worked in the computer industry, and the Spielbergs moved several times as he accepted new positions. They left Ohio for New Jersey in 1949, when Steven was three years old. Then, in 1957, Arnold Spielberg announced that the family, which now included three daughters, was going to Arizona.

Each move was difficult for Steven. He lost friends and

Although born in Cincinnati, Spielberg soon moved with his family to New Jersey, and later to Arizona. The longing for stability that he felt during these early years is reflected in his film *E.T.*, where a young boy finds an extraterrestrial and vows to keep it.

had to change schools. A little bit "nerdy," he did not always find making friends easy. He had big ears and a big nose, and his eyes bulged slightly, so some kids called him "Spielbug." Others made fun of him for being Jewish. He often felt lonely and afraid, and he feared that moving might make this even worse. Today, Spielberg says that his movie *E.T.* reflects some of these feelings of loneliness. "When Elliott finds E.T., he hangs onto E.T., he announces in no uncertain terms, 'I'm keeping him,' and he means it." Steven, too, wished he had something permanent to hold on to. Eventually, moviemaking became just that.

Leah Spielberg knew that Steven did not want to move to Arizona. To encourage him, she promised to buy him a horse—the perfect pet for what the Spielbergs thought of back then as "the Wild West." His mother never made good on her promise—and Steven still reminds her of that today. But although Steven did not want to go to Arizona, he ended up being happy there. In fact, he considers Arizona his "real home." For one thing, it was in Arizona that Steven first began making movies. Shortly after moving to Phoenix, he began playing with his father's movie camera.

Steven says that he became interested in making movies simply because there was a camera available to him. At the time, there were no video cameras for amateur use, but Arnold Spielberg had a little 8mm movie camera. The family often went camping, and he would record the trips on film. Steven remembers watching the movies and criticizing his father for the "shaky camera movements and bad exposures." Finally, his dad told Steven that he ought to film the movies himself if he thought he could do so much better.

From that point forward, Steven was the family photographer. But soon he realized that he could have a lot of fun with a movie camera. "I began to think that staging real life was much more exciting than just recording it," he recalls. "So I'd do things like forcing my parents to let me out of the car a hundred yards before we reached the campgrounds. . . . I'd run ahead and film them arriving and unpacking and pitching camp. . . . I began to actually stage the camping trips and later cut the bad footage out."

At the age of eleven, Steven made what he calls his first real film. He enjoyed staging make-believe wrecks using his train set, which often resulted in broken toys. Tired of having to fix them, his father finally said that if Steven broke the trains once more, he would take them away for good. Steven had a great idea: he would stage the biggest train wreck ever and film it with his dad's camera. "Then," remembers Steven, "I could look at my 8mm film over and over and enjoy the demolition of my trains without the threat of losing them." The result was a 3-minute-long film called *The Last Train Wreck*.

Being a Boy Scout also played a role in Steven's burgeoning career as a filmmaker. He enjoyed scouting and dreamed of becoming an Eagle Scout. To achieve this goal, a scout must earn twenty-one merit badges. Each merit badge is awarded for an accomplishment in one of a variety of different areas, and many are bestowed for athletic achievements. Steven was not much of an athlete, and he struggled to earn badges in activities such as swimming, canoeing, and running an obstacle course. When he needed to earn another merit badge, nothing appealed to him. Was there nothing that he would actually *enjoy* doing?

His father had an idea. Since Steven liked making movies so much, why not create a film to earn a merit badge? Although there was no badge for filmmaking, there was one for still photography. To earn the badge, a scout had to use photography to tell a story. Steven's scoutmaster agreed that if the boy made a short film, he would give him a photography merit badge.

So, in the summer of 1958, armed with his father's camera and three rolls of film, Steven went out into the Arizona desert to shoot a Western. His friends and fellow scouts starred in the film. The kids went to a restaurant, where an old red stagecoach was parked. Several of the "actors," including Steven's sister Anne, played passengers. In the movie, bandits wearing bandanas and carrying cap pistols overtake the stagecoach, stealing the passengers' belongings. Steven already knew how to fool the audience. He positioned the camera so that people watching the movie could not tell that there were no horses. And when one bandit was shot and thrown over a cliff, Steven used a dummy made of pillows, wearing clothes and shoes—and covered in ketchup for make-believe blood!

The other scouts already admired Steven's talent as a storyteller. Often they would gather around the campfire, and he would keep them entertained with ghost stories. Steven enjoyed telling stories and especially loved to scare people. When the Scouts saw his movie, they were even more impressed. Steven remembers how "the Boy Scouts cheered and applauded and laughed at what I did, and I really wanted to do that, to please again."

Steven continued his involvement with the Boy Scouts as an adult. In 1989 he was awarded the Distinguished Eagle Scout Award, an honor that he said was "the best memory of the entire year." At about that same time, he created a cinematography merit badge. Today, using Super 8 film or videotape, Boy Scouts can earn a badge the same way that Steven did years before. "Hopefully," Steven said, "it will do for some scouts what it did for me, which is to open up a whole lot of possibilities for discovering what talent you might possess."

Soon Steven was taking his camera along on every Scout trip. The boys always enjoyed seeing themselves on film. People not only loved watching his movies, but they delighted in starring in them, too. There was no limit to what Steven could film. He even hooked up a camera cart behind the family dog, a cocker spaniel named Thunder. The dog towed the cart around the neighborhood, and the result was a movie called *A Day in the Life of Thunder.*

Filmmaking was no longer just a hobby. By the age of twelve, Steven was already serious about making a career for himself as a movie director. "I knew after my third or fourth little 8mm epic that this was going to be a career, not just a hobby," he has said. He asked his father for a better camera, and Arnold Spielberg agreed. To earn money for all of his projects, Steven began renting movies and showing them to kids in the neighborhood. He printed tickets, and his sisters sold popcorn, candy, and drinks. There were no videos or DVDs in those days, so Steven used a film projector that Arnold brought home from work. He donated all of the money that he earned from admissions to a school for retarded children, but he kept the profits from the sales of concessions. After paying his sisters for their help, he applied the rest toward his filmmaking, paying for film, props, and other items that he needed to make his movies as professional as possible.

Arnold Spielberg had been a radio operator during World War II. Steven loved to hear his father's stories about his days as a soldier. His interest in the war soon led him into making war movies—and this interest would stay with him. Many years later, he directed two Academy Award-winning films about World War II, *Schindler's List* (1993) and *Saving Private Ryan* (1998). But Steven's first film on the same subject, *Fighter Squad,* was shot much earlier in his career, when he was thirteen years old.

With his father's help, Steven obtained permission to use the cockpit of a P-51 fighter plane parked at the Phoenix

At the young age of 13, Steven got permission to use a real P-51 fighter like this one to make his short film *Fighter Squad*. Although the plane never left the ground, the young director used a wind machine to create realistic effects.

airport. He used props, such as helmets, flags, and uniforms, donated by his father and other men in the neighborhood who had fought in the war. One of Steven's friends sat in the cockpit wearing a helmet, pretending to fly the plane. Steven stood on the wing filming the boy. If he wanted to show the plane turning, he would tilt the camera. A fan served as a wind machine. Steven wanted to show planes in flight, so he bought stock footage of fighter planes and spliced it into his film. Already his goal was to make realistic films with inspiring special effects.

In eighth grade, Steven made another Western. It was for a "career exploration" project at school, in which students talked about what they would like to do as adults. Steven showed the movie in class, and the other students loved it. Even his teacher was impressed. Clearly, Steven had a special talent. "I'm going to make movies," Steven announced to his class. "I'm going to direct and produce movies."

Spielberg's father, Arnold, had been a radio operator during World War II, and his stories inspired Steven's interest. While still a teenager, Steven made the war film *Escape to Nowhere*. Years later he would dazzle audiences with World War II films like *Schindler's List* and *Saving Private Ryan*.

Chapter **2**

The Big Break

STEVEN BEGAN SHOOTING another World War II story, *Escape to Nowhere,* in 1959, and it would take him until 1962 to complete it. But spending his weekends making movies was no sacrifice; it was a labor of love. It was also a way for this somewhat awkward teenager to make friends. "I discovered something I could do, and people would be interested in it and me," he recalled. By making movies, Steven created a circle of friends who admired him.

Steven even found a way to use filmmaking to tame one of the meanest kids at his school, Arcadia High. Steven was so afraid of this boy that he used to have nightmares about him. Sometimes the boy made insulting remarks about Steven's being Jewish. He went out of his way to torment Steven and the other "wimps" at school. One day, Steven had an idea. The boy looked a lot like John Wayne. What if he asked him to play the squadron leader in *Escape to Nowhere*?

At first the boy laughed at him, but he was flattered by the request. Soon he found himself acting under the direction of the nerd he had always harassed. Steven was still afraid of him. "But I was able to bring him over to a place where I felt safer: in front of the camera," he remembers. Steven realized that making movies not only made him feel good about himself, but it also gave him power.

Making *Escape to Nowhere* taught Steven how to use what he had available to him in his filmmaking endeavors. The Arizona desert provided a perfect location for his Westerns, and Steven found a way to use the setting in a war movie as well. He chose to focus the story on battles between German and American troops in the North African desert. Twenty or thirty boys volunteered to act in the battle scenes. To make the cast seem larger, they played both Germans and Americans. With only a limited supply of German army helmets, Steven directed his actors to dash past the camera and quickly hand their helmets to other boys, who then ran around behind the camera before making their appearance on film.

The Spielberg family got into the act as well. When Steven realized that he was short one actor for a scene, he grabbed his sister Anne and put her to work. She played a German soldier who was killed early in the action, so there would be little time for the audience to recognize that this particular soldier was a girl! Arnold Spielberg, dressed in army fatigues, drove the family's jeep, leading the infantry in its march across the desert. Leah Spielberg drove the jeep in a few scenes, too, dressed as a German soldier and wearing a helmet to disguise her gender.

The special effects are what really set this film apart from Steven's earlier efforts. In a 1980 interview, he proudly explained how he created the film's realistic battle scenes. "For shell explosions, I dug two holes in the ground and put a balancing board loaded with flour between them, then covered it with a bush. When a soldier ran over it, the flour made the perfect geyser in the air. Matter of fact, it works better than the gunpowder used in movies today."

When Steven won first place in the Arizona Amateur Film Contest for *Escape to Nowhere*, he received a number of books about filmmaking. Even better, he won a 16mm camera. Convinced that he already knew what the books could teach him, he donated them to the local library. Steven's father told him that film for the new camera would be more expensive than the 8mm film he had always used. He suggested that they trade it for a better 8mm camera. The camera that Steven ultimately chose had one very special feature: a sound system. Unlike today's video cameras, most movie cameras at that time did not record sound. So when Steven wanted to add sound to his films, he was forced to use a tape recorder. When he showed the movies, he would have to be very careful to start the tape at exactly the right moment so that it was in synch with the film. The new movie camera allowed him to record sound directly onto magnetic strips attached to the film, which would be a big advantage on his next undertaking, *Firelight*.

It took Steven and his cast and crew six months to complete *Firelight*. It was fortunate that Steven had a full-length movie on which to concentrate that year. His personal life was not all that easy. For one thing, he was doing poorly in school. Arnold Spielberg wanted his son to follow in his footsteps and become an engineer. Steven wanted nothing of the sort and spent his time not doing homework, but making movies, watching television, and reading science fiction, which caused friction between the two. Then, as Steven was working diligently on *Firelight,* he learned that his family was about to move again. "Just as I'd become accustomed to a school and a teacher and a best friend, the *for sale* sign would dig into the front yard."

The day after the premiere of *Firelight* at the Phoenix Little Theater, the Spielbergs moved to California. No matter how difficult it was to leave Arizona, moving to California did offer one important advantage: Steven was now that much closer to Hollywood. That proximity brought with it an exciting opportunity. The summer before he started his senior year of high school, he stayed in Southern California, where he worked as a clerical assistant at Universal Pictures. The year before, a family friend had introduced Steven to a man named Chuck Silvers, who worked in the editorial department at Universal. Chuck showed an interest in Steven, recognizing his great enthusiasm for the movie business. Silvers asked him to bring some of his films to show him. After viewing four of his films, he realized that Steven was no ordinary teenager. "With Steven," recalls Silvers, "nothing was impossible. That attitude came through. . . . At some point in time, it dawned on me that I was talking to somebody who had a burning ambition, and not only that, he was going to accomplish his mission."

In the summer of 1964, Silvers brought Steven into the editorial department to help out doing odd jobs. The work was far from the glamorous duties of a Hollywood movie director. He ran errands, sorted paperwork, and did all of the tasks that no one in the department wanted to do. But the job did give him the chance to see how a movie studio

Sadly, anti-Semitism (evidenced by these defaced Berlin shop windows) did not end with the defeat of the Nazis in World War II. A young Steven Spielberg encountered the ugly face of prejudice while attending high school in California.

works. "I visited every set I could, got to know people, observed techniques, and just generally absorbed the atmosphere." After such an exciting summer job, it would be difficult for anyone to go back to school. But Steven was hardly prepared for how tough his senior year would be.

The next fall, Steven started at Saratoga High School. Today, he calls that year "hell on earth." For the first time, Steven faced serious anti-Semitism—prejudice and hatred because of his Jewish heritage. People called him names and threw things at him. Some even punched him as they passed him in the hall. Years later he said, "The idea that a person would hit me because I was Jewish was startling to me."

Steven felt more like an outsider than he had ever had in his life. "It caused me great fear and an equal amount of shame."

Life at home was not peaceful either. His parents often fought. Arnold was a workaholic who spent little time at home. He worked late and traveled for his job. Leah was fun loving and artistic. "My mom and dad were so different," Steven has said. "They both love classical music and they both love my sisters and me. Aside from that, they [have] nothing in common." Over time, these differences had begun to make their marriage increasingly difficult. For several years, Steven and his sisters had overheard their parents arguing, talking of divorce. His sisters often grew tearful, and the four children would try to comfort each other.

Steven continued to make a few movies. At school he did what he could to fit in. He filmed football games for his high school and wrote sports stories for the school newspaper. He also made a playful documentary about Senior Sneak Day, an annual event for the graduating class. But, most of all, Steven tried to become serious about his studies. He wanted to be accepted into a good film school, such as the University of California at Los Angeles or the University of Southern California. When neither school accepted him, he chose California State College at Long Beach. The school did not have a film department, so he would have to study in the Department of Television and Radio. But the school did have one thing in its favor. It was close to Los Angeles and Universal Studios. In the end, Universal Studios would become Steven's film school.

Steven's parents broke up soon after he graduated from high school. Leah and the girls returned to Arizona, and Steven and his father moved to Los Angeles, where Steven could easily commute to school and to Universal Studios. Steven still was not very interested in school. One professor recalled that Steven knew more about cameras than the professors did; he should have been teaching some of the classes rather than attending them. So Steven spent two days a week at school, putting in only minimal effort. The other three days of the work week were spent at Universal, hoping to meet as many important people as he could.

Steven's father was still frustrated by his son's lack of interest in school. He even called Chuck Silvers, hoping Steven's mentor might encourage him to work harder in college. Silvers said that he could do no such thing. He understood that Steven's goal was to become a movie director, and he believed that he possessed the talent to make that dream come true. He told Arnold Spielberg that Steven would need a big break to make it as a Hollywood director. The best chance at getting a break would be to spend as much time as he could at Universal. "They don't care whether he's got a degree," Silvers said. "They're interested in what he can put on screen."

Today, Steven says that while working harder in college might have delayed his career by a few years, he regrets having paid so little attention to his studies. "I think I would have had a much more well-rounded education," he says. But, at the time, Steven could not find the motivation to study. He and his father would never see eye to eye on the subject, so he decided that it was time to leave home. He moved into an apartment with a friend named Ralph Burris.

Friends remember that Steven almost always had a camera with him in those days, and Steven himself says that he did little during college except "watch movies and make movies." But no matter how hard he tried, Steven had a difficult time finding anyone at Universal who would look at his work. When he would ask someone to watch one of his 8mm films, they would tell him they would not waste their time on anything less than 16mm—and 35mm would be even better.

Steven took this advice seriously. In 1967 he decided that it was time to make his first 35mm film, but he knew that the project would be neither easy nor inexpensive. Still, he needed something to demonstrate his talent to the people at Universal. His roommate, Ralph, was intrigued by Steven and by the movie business. He dropped out of school, hoping to jumpstart his own a career as a producer, and convinced his parents to contribute $3,000 to Steven's movie. (A producer is the person in charge of making a film, including choosing the screenwriter and director and planning the budget and schedule.) The two set to work on *Slipstream,* an action movie about bicycle racing. Steven found other sources of support as well. Even though his father was still worried about Steven's direction in life, he agreed to help pay for rental equipment, such as the 35mm camera and a crane. Chuck Silvers and others at Universal gave him "short ends" of film reels, which were pieces of unused film that he could splice together and use to shoot much of the movie.

Perhaps most important, he found people who were willing to help him. Steven asked a cameraman named Allen Daviau to shoot the film. Daviau would go on to be the cinematographer for several of Steven's films, including *The Color Purple* and *E.T.* Daviau was not very experienced with 35mm film at the time, so he asked another cameraman to run the first camera, and he ran the second. Steven also convinced members of bicycle-racing clubs to take part in the film. They drove to the desert with their bicycles in tow, agreeing to do whatever the director asked of them.

After several weeks of shooting, Steven had only the start and finish of the race left to shoot. But money was running out. They could afford to rent the equipment for only one more weekend. After finding the perfect location and scheduling the shoot, Steven rounded up a huge number of people to play cyclists and spectators. Unfortunately, on the weekend of the shoot, the skies opened up, and rain flooded the site that Steven had chosen. With no money left, he could not finish the film. Steven and the rest of the crew were disappointed. But Steven had no intention of giving up.

In early 1968, Steven met an aspiring producer who was willing to pay the production costs for a short film. Steven proposed a story to him about a young couple who hitchhikes from the Southern California desert to the ocean. They fall in love but finally drift apart. The producer liked the idea but suggested they do it without dialogue to save money. The movie would have only music to accompany the action. Steven agreed, certain that he could tell the story through pictures. The name of the movie was *Amblin'*.

Steven shot more than three hours of film for what was supposed to be a short feature, which meant that he had to edit the film. (To edit a film is to cut out everything except what is essential to the story and then put the scenes in the most logical sequence.) Once he had cut the film to twenty-six minutes, he added the soundtrack. The process took him six weeks, working seven days a week from four in the afternoon until four in the morning. Finally, his showcase film was ready. And the first person he wanted to show it to was Chuck Silvers.

The "big break" that Silvers had talked about a few years before was about to happen. "When I saw *Amblin'*," Silvers said, "I cried. It was everything it should have been. It was perfect." Silvers thought about what to do and decided that the best way for Steven to get his foot in the door would be

As a clerical assistant at Hollywood's Universal Studios, Spielberg was at last within reach of the movie business he loved. With the help of Universal's Chuck Silvers, Spielberg got his first big break —not in movies but TV.

to start in television. Silvers contacted Sidney J. Sheinberg, vice president of production for Universal TV. Sheinberg was a busy man, and it would not be easy to talk him into looking at the film, but Silvers did what he could to persuade him. "Sid, I've got something I want you to see," Silvers said. "If you don't look at this, somebody else will."

Something Silvers said must have convinced the vice president that *Amblin'* was not a film that he should miss—and that Steven Spielberg was not a talent that he could afford to overlook. Even though he had a stack of work by would-be filmmakers waiting to be watched, Sheinberg trusted Silvers's judgment. He watched *Amblin',* and the next day he asked Silvers to set up a meeting with the young filmmaker.

Within one week, Steven had a seven-year contract with Universal to direct television shows, with the possibility of directing movies in the future. Steven went straight to Silvers to tell him the good news. He asked what he could do for him in return. Silvers responded that he could do two things for him. "When you make it big, you can be nice to young people," Silvers said. And Steven has kept that promise, helping a long list of first-time directors and producers. But Steven wanted to do something more personal for Silvers. "What do *you* want?" he asked. Silvers replied, "Every time we meet I would like a hug." According to Silvers, Steven has kept this second promise as well. "Whenever I see him, he gives me a hug."

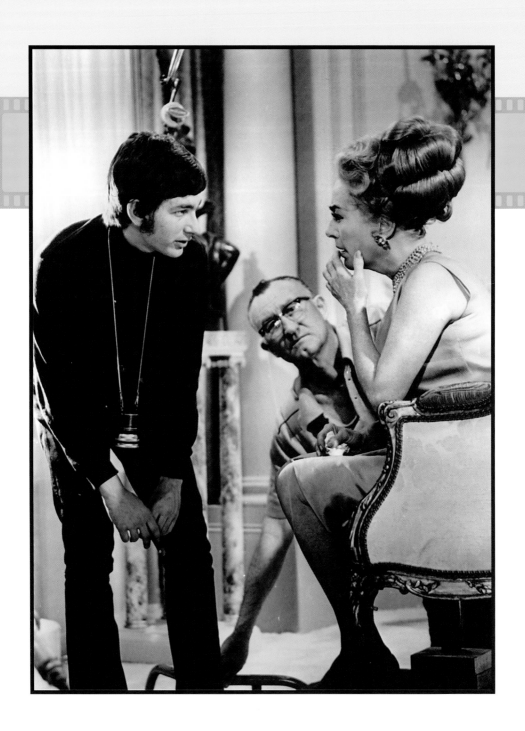

One of Spielberg's first big challenges was directing noted film star Joan Crawford in a TV episode of *Night Gallery*. Steven applied his dedication and talent to the project and soon won the respect of Crawford and the crew.

Chapter 3

A Young Man in Hollywood

WHEN STEVEN ARRIVED in Hollywood to begin his career, he was different from other people in the movie business. At the time, most filmmakers and studio executives were much older than he was. Few young people could get their feet in the door at the major Hollywood studios. A little luck and a lot of talent had brought Steven the break that he had hoped for—and at a very young age. But it would take a little time before he would be granted the chance to direct the films that he dreamed of making.

At first, Steven had very little to do at Universal. No one

seemed interested in offering him a project. It may have seemed like a lifetime before he received his first assignment, but it was actually just six weeks from the day that he had signed his contract. It did not involve a feature film for theaters as he would have liked, but one segment of a television movie called *Night Gallery,* which consisted of three short episodes. The episode that he would direct was titled "Eyes."

Choosing Steven to direct this segment showed that Universal's leaders had faith in him, not because the film itself was so important but because one of its stars was a major Hollywood actress named Joan Crawford. By this time, Crawford was sixty-three years old. She had been starring in films since the 1920s. Imagine her surprise, after having worked with some of the most famous directors in Hollywood, to learn that she would be working with a 23-year-old rookie!

"Eyes" tells the story of a blind woman who blackmails a surgeon into removing a poor man's eyes and transplanting them into her so that she can see once more, with the knowledge that her vision will last for only a few hours. On the night after the surgery, just as the bandages are removed, there is a blackout. All of New York City is left in total darkness, and the woman can see nothing. Tormented by what has happened, she goes insane. Steven was not thrilled with the script, but he knew how important it was to prove himself as a director. He dedicated himself to creating the best possible work that he could.

Crawford played the part of the blind woman. She was kind and friendly to Steven and even asked his advice about how to interpret certain scenes. Steven said that she treated him like a professional, "like I'd been working for fifty years." But the crew was less friendly to their young director. He was nervous, having never met them before, and they did nothing to put him at ease. "I came on the set, and they thought it was a joke. . . . I really couldn't get anybody to take me seriously for two days. It was very embarrassing." Steven knew that if he failed to do a good job on this first assignment, it could very well be his last.

Under these difficult circumstances, Steven forged ahead. To gain the confidence of the crew, he did his best to prove that he was a professional. He prepared for filming by creating storyboards. (Storyboards are drawings that show all of the scenes in the order in which they will occur.) Using them, he could visualize the entire story as they worked. Even as a young man, Steven had an excellent sense of his own filmmaking style, and the crew could see this. They were impressed by some of the challenging shots that he filmed. After his early difficulties, his professional attitude and skill helped the crew to accept him.

One of a director's most important responsibilities is staying on schedule. Every day past deadline costs the studio money. By the time Steven finished shooting his episode, he was two days behind—a big deal for what was supposed to take less than a week. The first delay came when Ms. Crawford missed a day of work because she was ill. When she returned to work, she had difficulty with a scene. She was so upset that Steven canceled shooting to help her practice the scene. Even though the lost time was not his fault, Steven feared that the studio executives would blame him. The pressure of making "Eyes" left him disillusioned with the business of filmmaking.

When "Eyes" was aired on NBC, it received mixed reviews from the critics. One called Steven's directing "topnotch," but others were not as kind. Some said that he was too "artsy" for television, shooting too many difficult and unusual shots. Others contended that he was simply too young to direct—and that his work was the proof. Steven felt terrible. In fact, he wondered if he was in the wrong business. "The pressure of that show was just too much for me. . . . I really felt this wasn't the business I wanted to be in."

It would be eight months before he was given another chance to direct. In that time, he suggested ideas to Universal's studio heads, but no one was interested in them. He decided to take a few months off to concentrate on writing scripts; he showed his work to Universal and other studios but found no opportunities. One problem was that Steven insisted that he should be the one to direct his scripts. Most executives were unsure of this young director. After all, they reasoned, he had completed only one professional film so far.

Desperate to get back to work, Steven returned to Universal. He was eager to take on any project, just to get behind the camera again, which meant was that he had to be willing to direct more television programs, even though he really wanted to make feature films. But Steven realized that he had to pay his dues before he could convince studio leaders to let him take on bigger and better projects. For the next three years, he directed numerous television shows, including episodes of *Columbo* and *Marcus Welby, M.D.,* two popular programs of the day.

Steven found that television could provide him with the experience he needed to move his career forward. "I found that TV taught me how to do homework," he said in a 1982 interview. "It taught me how to sketch out ideas. . . . I'm really happy to have started in a disciplined area such as television." But, at the same time, the work was not what he really dreamed of doing. It was not an art form, but a job.

Still, with each new program that he directed, he learned a little bit more about what it meant to be a director. He earned a strong reputation and received excellent reviews for his work. As people started to take note, he began to be offered more interesting opportunities—and eventually more influence. The first sign that directors have "made it" is when they begin to direct projects of their choosing. In Steven's case, the first of these was a television movie called *Duel.*

Duel is based on a short story by science-fiction writer Richard Matheson that Steven had read and immediately wanted to make into a feature film. It tells the tale of a man in a car who is chased for miles by a truck driver, who tries time and again to push him off the road. Universal bought the film rights to the story, and Matheson was hired to write the script. At first, the writer worried that the short story could not be made into a full-length movie. Steven, too, was faced with a great challenge: How would he keep *Duel* from becoming repetitive, considering that the film is really little more than a very long chase scene across long stretches of California highway?

Steven had a brilliant idea. In the past, he had always counted on storyboards to help him to visualize a story as he worked. For *Duel* he came up with a different way of achieving the same end. He hired an artist to create a gigantic map, forty feet long and five feet tall, of the road on which the chase was to take place. Steven described it as a "mural of the movie" that he could use to plot the film's action, scene by scene. He wrote notes on the map describing each shot, such as "this is where the truck passes the car and then the car passes the truck." While shooting the film, he and the crew used it as an overview of the script. Steven has said that the film should have

In Spielberg's first Hollywood film, *Duel,* actor Dennis Weaver plays a driver tormented by a phantom truck in the desert. Using little dialogue and never showing the face of the truck driver, Spielberg created a tense and compelling film that impressed both audiences and film executives.

taken up to fifty days to shoot, but the map allowed him to complete it in just sixteen.

One of the most frightening things about *Duel* is that the viewer never sees the truck driver, just his arm hanging out of the window, his cowboy boots, and the terrifying image of the monster-like gasoline tanker that Steven chose "to play" the truck. One never knows exactly why the driver has decided to challenge the man in the car, and in a way, the truck becomes the villain. Extreme close-ups of the car's driver, played by actor Dennis Weaver, show his panic. Steven used a wide-angle lens to shoot the truck, which artificially shortens the distance between it and the car. He also chose camera angles that made the truck assume what he called "Godzilla proportions." These and other techniques made *Duel* a suspense-filled thriller right to the end, when Dennis Weaver's character finally manages to force the truck over a cliff.

Duel aired on November 8, 1971, barely a month after Steven finished filming it, and won rave reviews. Almost immediately, Steven began to receive offers to direct feature films. An expanded version of the film was released in theaters in Europe, Australia, and Japan. It was a success, earning Steven an international reputation as a bright young director to watch.

However, even as the pieces of his career seemed to be falling into place, Steven was still under contract to do more television work for Universal. The fact that he was receiving offers to direct feature films made satisfying this obligation all the more difficult. Steven later recalled that while he was directing television, he "wasn't getting any of that stimulation, that gratification that I . . . got making 8mm war movies when I was twelve years old. I didn't have that passion. . . . It's only when I got into feature films—actually when I got into TV movies and made *Duel* —that I kind of rediscovered the fun about making films." Fortunately, he would not have to wait much longer to pursue his dream. He directed a few more television programs for Universal before finally taking on his first feature film, *The Sugarland Express*.

Back in 1969, Steven had seen a newspaper article about a former convict named Bobby Dent and his wife, Ila Faye. The opening paragraph read, "An ex-convict, freed just two weeks ago and willing to do anything 'to talk to his kids and love them,' kidnapped a Texas highway patrolman in his squad car today in a high-speed chase that ended seven hours later in a gunfight with lawmen." The trio drove several hundred miles across southern Texas, followed by a reported one hundred police cars, before the chase ended in a shootout—and Dent's death. What Hollywood director could fail to see that this was a story just waiting to be put on film?

In 1969, after completing "Eyes," Steven had tried to convince Universal to let him make Dent's story into a movie. No one at the studio believed that people wanted to see such a depressing story. Disappointed, Steven tucked the story away in the back of his mind, hoping to day revive it. Three years later, a hot director after the critical success of *Duel,* he pitched the story to Universal once again. This time the studio agreed. Steven and two screenwriters, Hal Barwood and Matthew Robbins, set to work immediately.

Steven and the writers changed the story for the screen. In the newspaper clipping that he had read, Ila Faye Dent was only mentioned in passing. Steven believed that she should be the main character of the film, and he changed her name to Lou Jean Poplin. In the film, the couple's son has been taken to a foster home. Lou Jean desperately wants her son back and convinces her husband to escape from jail, even though just four months remain of his sentence, to help her take him from the foster home. Lou Jean is motivated not only by a mother's love, but also by a reckless obsession. She tries so hard to get the child back because she knows that she has been a terrible parent. Ultimately, her actions result in the death of her husband. The film's title comes from the name of the fictional Texas town where the film ends, Sugarland.

Universal insisted that Spielberg and his producers find a major female star to accept the role, hoping to thereby ensure the film's success. Goldie Hawn was Steven's choice, although she was best known as the ditzy blonde star of the television comedy show, *Laugh In*. Hawn, however, had won an Oscar for her performance in the film *Cactus Flower,* and Steven was certain that she could play Lou Jean. Hawn agreed to do *The Sugarland Express*, in part because she was excited about working with its director. "Think of the career Steven's got ahead of him," she said.

On *The Sugarland Express,* 26-year-old Steven would be working with a larger, more experienced crew than ever before. The producer, Richard Zanuck, had asked the crew to start slowly and to not expect too much from their director on the first day. Zanuck planned to show up on the set late that day, wanting Steven to feel that he was in charge. By the time he arrived, Steven had set up what Zanuck called "the most complex shot I've ever seen in my life! . . . I knew right then and there, when I saw him in action, that he knew what he was doing." From the very first day of shooting, the crew knew that they were working with a professional.

Steven and his cameraman, Vilmos Zsigmond, wanted the film to have a realistic, "documentary feeling." They shot as much of the film as possible using natural light and live sound. Many filmmakers use a technique called process photography when they shoot actors in moving cars. (With process photography, the background of the scene is filmed first, then the actors are shot in front of this filmed background, projected onto a process screen. The purpose is to create the illusion that the actors are actually in the same scene as the background.) Steven did not think this looked real, so he came up with a new way to film the action inside the car. First, he removed the wheels from the vehicle. Then, he mounted the car on a trailer, sitting close to the ground. The crew attached a

Based on the real-life story of convict Bobby Dent, *The Sugarland Express* marked Spielberg's first big film project for Universal. Although the film scored poorly at the box office, Spielberg's dynamic directing earned the praise of both *The New Yorker* and *Newsweek*.

platform to the trailer, from which Steven and Zsigmond could film the car as it moved. With the help of a quiet new camera, they were also able to shoot scenes from inside the car.

One factor that drew Steven to the story was the chance to film the biggest car chase ever put on film. The real-life chase had involved about one hundred police cars. Steven's budget only allowed them to use about forty vehicles in *Sugarland*. He had to figure out a way to make those forty cars look like one hundred. He also knew that, even with forty cars, viewers would see only the first few cars unless he shot from high above ground; otherwise, everything after the first four or five cars would disappear on the horizon. Filming shots from a cherry picker, Steven and Zsigmond managed to capture on film a seemingly endless line of police cars chasing the fugitives. "I employed long lenses to compact the line of vehicles in one tight plane of action," Spielberg explained. "There's a lot of wasted production value in having forty-five patrol cars when you can only see the first seven or eight and the rest taper into the horizon line and vanish. So the long lens was an invaluable aid in making forty-five cars look like one hundred."

Together, Steven and Zsigmond accomplished feats that had never been done on film before. At the same time, Steven never let the excitement of the chase outweigh the emotional impact of the film's story. Critics praised him both for his technique and for his exploration of the characters. When the film appeared in April 1974, Pauline Kael, the respected *New Yorker* magazine film critic, said, "This is one of the most phenomenal debut films in the history of movies." *Newsweek*'s critic hailed "the arrival of an extraordinarily talented new filmmaker."

Unfortunately, *The Sugarland Express* did not do well at the box office. Moviegoers did not want to see perky Goldie Hawn in such a somber film. Many came expecting a comedy but were faced with a movie that was deadly serious. "It did get good reviews," Steven said, "but I would have given away all those reviews for a bigger audience." Attracting a big audience with an entertaining movie would be a major focus of Steven's career, and that big audience would soon come. As he received the bad news about *Sugarland,* he was already at work on his next film—a movie called *Jaws.*

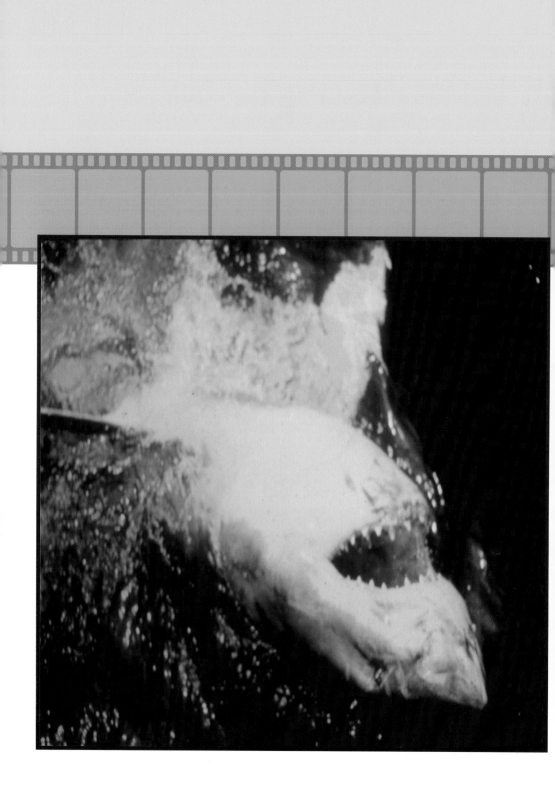

Now regarded as a terror-movie classic, *Jaws* told the story of a shore community's battle against a man-eating shark. With delays and cost overruns, the film turned out to be the most demanding project Spielberg had ever undertaken.

Fear, Fantasy, and Adventure

IN APRIL 1974, as *The Sugarland Express* hit movie theaters across the United States, Steven Spielberg was on the Massachusetts island of Martha's Vineyard. He was there to begin shooting *Jaws,* a film based on the best-selling novel by Peter Benchley. This movie would be among the most technically difficult projects of Steven's career.

Jaws is the story of a great white shark that feeds on human prey off the coast of Long Island, New York. As a boy, author Peter Benchley had spent summers on the island of Nantucket. He and his father and brothers went on shark-fishing trips.

From a young age, Benchley knew how terrifying these sea creatures could be. As an adult, in the summer of 1964, the idea for a novel about a murderous great white shark came to him when he read the story of a fisherman who had harpooned a gigantic 4,500-pound shark. He began to create a character, Captain Quint, based on this man. It took some time for the story to come to him, but in 1971 he sold the idea to a publisher and set to work on his first novel.

The story was so frightening that even before the book had been published, moviemakers had begun to talk about bringing it to the screen. Although several studios expressed strong interest in buying the rights from Benchley, Universal producers Richard Zanuck and David Brown convinced him that they would make the best film from his book.

Zanuck and Brown did not immediately think of Spielberg when trying to choose the best director for *Jaws,* although they were working with him on *The Sugarland Express.* They knew that shooting a film on the ocean would be difficult and would require an experienced hand. One Universal executive suggested the legendary master of suspense Alfred Hitchcock as the best director for the project. Other high-profile filmmakers were considered as well. But, all along, Spielberg wanted the project for himself. He found the novel's finale exhilarating, as the three main characters go off to hunt the great white shark. He was intrigued by the idea of how three men, against each other at the beginning of the story, must join forces to fight something more powerful than they are.

Perhaps another reason that Steven wanted to make the movie was to scare people. As a boy, he had loved frightening his two younger sisters, often to the point of giving them nightmares. He had also greatly enjoyed telling ghost stories to his fellow Boy Scouts. Making *Jaws* would allow him to scare moviegoers all over the world. "*Jaws* is a horror story about a great white shark," Steven said in a 1974 interview. "But it's really a movie about our fear of the water. When you're out swimming . . . half of your body is under the surface and you can't keep tabs on what's happening down there around your feet. *Jaws* will scare the hell out of anyone who's ever swum in the ocean!"

Finally, Zanuck and Brown decided that, as a young director with new ideas, Steven might be just the person to bring visual excitement to the story. In June 1973 they announced that he would be the director to tackle the tale of a man-eating shark.

Just as Steven landed the job that he had hoped for, he began to have second thoughts. For one thing, he realized that it would be a very difficult project. It would be impossible to work with a live shark—or even to find one as big as the creature from Benchley's novel. How could he make a fake shark seem real? Steven realized that it was much easier to tell the story in a book, where the reader's imagination creates the shark, than to figure out how to put such a creature on film.

Steven also worried that making such an action-packed thriller might not be the best choice for his career. He knew that *Jaws* was primarily a commercial movie, not necessarily one that would further his reputation as a gifted filmmaker. Would people think of him as an action director who specialized in tales of people fighting against powerful, inhuman killers—first a truck in *Duel,* now a shark in *Jaws?*

With these concerns in mind, Steven set to work on *Jaws* in the spring of 1974. He was right to worry that it would be a tough film to make. Twenty years later, Bill Gilmore, the film's production manager, recalled that it was "the most difficult film ever made, to this day." In the end, *Jaws* was much more of a challenge than anyone could have imagined. It cost double the amount that the filmmakers had budgeted. It also took three times as long as anticipated to make; the producers had planned to shoot the film in 55 days, but it took 159.

As shooting was about to begin, casting had yet to be completed. Steven wanted actor Richard Dreyfuss to play the part of the ichthyologist (marine scientist) Matt Hooper. Dreyfuss was not interested and thought that the script was terrible. Just before the cameras rolled, he finally agreed to take the part, although he still did not believe that it would be a good film. Steven also had a difficult time finding the right people to play Captain Quint and the town police chief, Brody. He finally selected Robert Shaw to play Quint and cast Roy Schieder as Brody.

Then, on the very day that shooting was to begin, the script was not ready. Like Dreyfuss, Steven was not pleased with script. In fact, he stated publicly that he had not liked the book—his only interest was in its final 120 pages, the exciting finale. Peter Benchley had been hired to write the screenplay, but Steven and the producers were not satisfied with either of the two drafts that he produced.

Steven began looking for another writer. He hired Carl Gottlieb, who came to Martha's Vineyard and shared a house with Steven. Each night, after filming, the two men worked to rewrite the pages of the script that would be shot the next day. Sometimes the actors would offer their contributions as well. Gottlieb continued to work after Steven went to sleep. The next morning, he would give the pages to a typist. By 8:30 A.M., the pages had to be approved and ready for filming.

As if these dilemmas were not enough, the technical aspects of making the film presented great difficulties from

To create the suspense needed for *Jaws,* Spielberg decided not to show the shark on screen until well into the film. The technique worked, and *Jaws* went on to become a huge hit.

the very beginning. In fact, there were so many production problems that the crew members jokingly called the film *Flaws.* Shooting on water was among the most challenging aspects of making the film. Steven had resisted shooting process photography in *The Sugarland Express,* and he had not changed his opinion about this technique. At the time, most movies set on the ocean were shot in a huge water tank with the sea projected onto a process screen. Steven believed that the audience could tell that what was being shown was not real, and he wanted no part of that. *Jaws* would be shot on the Atlantic Ocean, even though no one had ever made a movie at sea in a small boat. The film's producers agreed, not knowing how challenging their task would turn out to be.

For one thing, the weather on the sea changes constantly. Storms forced the crew to postpone shooting. Sometimes they would have to shoot parts of the same scene on two different days. One day would be sunny, the next cloudy and gray. Steven, the cast, and the crew would have to wait for another sunny day to shoot again, or else the audience would be able to tell that the scene did not take place in a single day.

Another problem was that the scenes of the shark hunt were supposed to occur far out at sea. The three characters are in a small boat, the *Orca*. Its radio is broken, and there are no other ships for miles. No one can help them. Steven believed that this scenario is what made the story exciting. But during the summer the waters surrounding Martha's Vineyard are crowded with vacationers on their sailboats. When a boat appeared in the background, Steven and his crew would have to stop shooting, ask the people on the boat to move, and then wait, causing numerous delays. Sometimes the boaters would refuse to leave, increasing the delays still further. Nonetheless, shooting *Jaws* on the water made a big difference in how the film turned out. As Gilmore noted, "Despite all the problems it caused us, ultimately it's why the picture was so incredibly successful, because everybody was *there*. It was a real sea and a real boat."

Of all the problems faced by the cast and crew of *Jaws*, nothing, however, compared to the three mechanical sharks, nicknamed "Bruce," that had been built for the film.

To make the sharks, the producers hired a special-effects artist named Bob Mattey, who had created a giant squid for a Disney film called *20,000 Leagues Under the Sea.* Once the sharks arrived on the set, the trouble began. One shark sank. Another exploded. The one that remained did not work. No one had tested 12-ton Bruce in ocean water. Salt water ate away at the structure and its mechanical system. When Steven saw the first footage of the shark, he was miserable, noting that "Bruce's eyes crossed, and his jaw wouldn't close right." How could they expect anyone to believe that this was a real shark?

Mattey and his assistants worked to improve Bruce, but the shark was not ready until late in the summer. Even then, it did not always work. To deal with this unfortunate situation, Steven came up with an idea. He decided that it might be even scarier to suggest the shark's presence rather than to actually show it. In other words, it would be more frightening *not* to see the shark. In so doing, he created a more suspenseful—and terrifying— movie. "I think that the collective audience has a better, broader imagination than I do," said Steven. He believed that they would see "a much more horrific shark in their heads when I suggested an occurrence below the surface than I provided with the rubber shark." And he was right. As moviegoers watched *Jaws,* they were never sure where the shark was, or when this invisible demon would come charging out of the water. And when it did, the audience invariably screamed. As it turned out, the very thing that had caused so many problems ended up being largely responsible for the movie's success.

Finally, 159 days and $10 million later, filming at last came to an end. The cast and crew were exhausted and miserable, and Steven was worried. "I thought my career as a filmmaker was over," he said. "I heard rumors from back in Hollywood that I would never work again because no one had ever taken a film a hundred days over schedule— let alone a director whose first picture had failed at the box office."

Still, the project was not over. The next step was taking the film into the editing room. Verna Fields was the editor for *Jaws*. Together, she and Steven fine-tuned the film and determined the sequence in which the scenes would appear. Some people in the movie industry, and film critics as well, have suggested that Fields "saved" the movie. But many, including Steven himself, felt that she took too much credit for the work. Writer Carl Gottlieb said, "The film didn't need saving." As she accepted an Academy Award for her contribution to *Jaws,* Fields herself said that Steven "delivered so much good footage that it became an editor's dream." Ultimately, if Steven had not shot the film, there would have been nothing for Fields to work with.

When Universal executives viewed an early version (or "rough cut") of *Jaws*, no one was very impressed with it. Zanuck and Brown were worried, but they knew that there was still work to be done. For one thing, most of the under-water scenes still had to be shot and edited into the film. Perhaps more important, there was no score. (The music that accompanies a film is known as a score. A film's score makes a major contribution to the overall work.) In the case of *Jaws,* before music was added one could hear the funny sounds the mechanical shark made. Would people laugh at the creature instead fearing it?

The score for *Jaws* did much more than simply cover up strange noises, however. Composer John Williams created the famous score. Williams had worked with Steven on *The Sugarland Express,* and the two would collaborate for

Part of what made *Jaws* so frightening was the use of music in the soundtrack. Composer John Williams (seen here) brought his talents to the task and created a theme that sent chills through audiences worldwide.

many years to come. In fact, Williams has created some of the most memorable film scores of all time, many for Steven Spielberg movies. But the music from *Jaws* may be among the most recognizable movie themes of all time.

Williams's score creates tension and helps to suggest the presence of the unseen shark. At first, Steven thought that the simple but terrifying 4-note theme was too "primitive." In fact, he laughed when Williams played it for him for the first time. But Williams told him that he was serious. "I mean it," he said. "This is *Jaws*." He convinced Steven, and he was absolutely right. *Jaws* "was a good picture before it was scored," noted editor Verna Fields, but the "score did tremendous things for it."

Jaws opened in June 1975. Within fourteen days, it had made a profit. Within sixty-four days, it had broken box-office records and become the most successful film in motion-picture history, bumping Francis Ford Coppola's *The Godfather* out of the lead. (Two years later, George Lucas's *Star Wars* would take over this title.) In the end, it earned $458 million internationally—a remarkable feat given the difficulty of its history.

The critics had mixed opinions about the film. One praised Steven, saying, "It speaks well of this director's gifts that some of the most frightening sequences in *Jaws* are those where we don't even see the shark." But another said that she did not feel she had "to give it a rave review because I jumped out of my seat. . . . You feel like a rat, being given shock treatment." The greater the film's success, the more people began to discredit it. "For the first twelve weeks," Steven noted, "people were thrilled by it. Six months later they were saying that no film that made that amount of money could be that good."

Steven would face this type of criticism for some time to come. Over the years, people would criticize him for being more interested in making hugely successful movies that appealed to the biggest possible audience than with creating carefully crafted films worthy of his talent. But, at twenty-eight years old, Steven Spielberg was a millionaire. He had made the most successful film of all time. And, most important, the film's success gave him the creative freedom that he had long desired.

While Steven was working on *Jaws,* he had already begun to think about his next film. As it turned out, Columbia Pictures was interested in his dream project—a movie he would call *Close Encounters of the Third Kind.* He had wanted to make a film about unidentified flying objects (UFOs) for years. Unlike the science-fiction films he remembered from his childhood, in which aliens were evil creatures bent on destroying Earth, Steven wanted to depict extraterrestrial life forms as friendly, benevolent beings. He wrote the script himself, basing it on *Firelight,* the feature film he had made as a teenager. "I would have gone to great lengths to make it," he later said of *Close Encounters.*

The title for the film refers to what UFO believers consider the three kinds of encounters with extraterrestrial life. An encounter of the first kind is a UFO sighting. The second kind requires physical evidence that UFOs exist. The third is actual contact and communication with alien life. *Close Encounters of the Third Kind* tells the story of an ordinary man named Roy Neary, played by Richard Dreyfuss, who first comes into contact with a UFO during a blackout, changing his life forever. He somehow knows that aliens will come to Earth, and he is driven to communicate with them. Like many Spielberg films, *Close Encounters* features an ordinary man—"Mr. Everyday Regular Fella," as Steven has called him—faced with an extraordinary situation.

As Roy's obsession with extraterrestrial life grows more intense, he argues with his wife, who thinks that he has gone crazy. He decides that he must find the mystical mountain where he is certain that the aliens will land. Ultimately, he leaves his family to search for it. In the end, he locates the mothership. Roy and others who have gathered communicate with the aliens using music—the famous five-note motif written for the film by John Williams. At the movie's end, Roy is escorted onto the ship by the childlike aliens, having made the decision to go with them.

From the start, Steven knew that his film would only be popular if people did not fear the aliens. He thought that many people truly wanted to believe in life on other planets and that his film should inspire hope. For this reason, it was vital that the aliens look just right. Usually, aliens in movies were portrayed by people in costume, but Steven thought that there might be ways to make them more realistic. First, he brought a chimpanzee to the set and dressed him in an alien costume—a large head made of latex and a "flimsy ballerina costume." Then, the crew put the chimp on roller skates because Steven did not want the alien to walk like a primate but to glide. They put the chimp on a ramp, and he immediately slid and fell down. The chimp continued to play, laughing and having a good time. Finally, he pulled off the latex head and threw it at the crew. Clearly, they had to find another way!

Steven still was not convinced that actors in costume was the best option. The crew worked to create perfect models for the aliens that would look real. Once they were satisfied, cameraman Vilmos Zsigmond overexposed the images of the aliens so that they could barely be seen. The result was magical. The lead alien, nicknamed "Puck," had to be able to make much more intricate movements than did the other beings. He was created by the combined efforts of a marionette maker and a gifted Italian artist, Carlo Rambaldi, who painstakingly crafted Puck's face, complete with its ability to smile. It took eight people to operate the cable mechanisms that controlled Puck, but the effect was dazzling.

The film's state-of-the-art special effects, especially

Encouraged by the success of *Jaws,* Spielberg tackled his next project, *Close Encounters of the Third Kind,* a tale of alien visitors that involved exciting special effects. Although the film's budget ran well beyond studio expectations, *Close Encounters* garnered Spielberg his first Oscar nomination.

during the scene in which the mothership lands on Earth, were unlike anything moviegoers had seen before. This meant that *Close Encounters* was a very expensive film to make—to the tune of $19 million. The budget had been set at just over $4 million. Once again, Steven had gone over budget, but this time he had the success of *Jaws* to back him up. Still, he worried about whether the movie would be a success—and whether the studio would be able to earn back its investment. Would enough people want to see his latest film? He was not sure that he could expect another big hit like *Jaws.*

When *Close Encounters* entered theaters in November 1977, it had one difficult hurdle to overcome: *Star Wars,* the mega-hit by Steven's friend George Lucas. *Star Wars* had been released earlier that year and quickly had become the most popular film of all time. People waited in long lines for tickets, and it sold out in every theater where it played. Some people saw it five, ten, even twenty times in a single summer. No one had ever seen anything like it. Steven felt that *Star Wars,* also a science-fiction flick, was his and *Close Encounters'* rival. Not only had it surpassed the box-office record of *Jaws,* but, because it had come out before *Close Encounters,* Steven feared that it would take away much of that film's audience.

Steven should not have wasted time worrying. The film was an immediate hit, and it eventually earned $270 million. Perhaps *Star Wars* had made moviegoers hungry for more tales of life beyond planet Earth. *Close Encounters* also received great reviews. Said *Time* magazine reviewer Frank Rich, "*Close Encounters* offers proof, if any were needed, that Spielberg's reputation is no accident. His new movie is richer than *Jaws,* and it reaches the viewer at a far more profound level than *Star Wars.*" Although a few reviewers worried that Steven was more of a technical wizard than a gifted filmmaker, many believed that *Close Encounters* represented a turning point in his career, representing his desire to make more personal, emotional films.

With *Close Encounters,* Steven received his first Oscar nomination for best director, one of the eight nominations that the film received. He lost to Woody Allen, who won the award for *Annie Hall.* The movie did win two Oscars, however, one for cinematography (motion picture photography) and one for sound-effects editing.

While Steven must have been disappointed by the loss, the praise of critics eased the pain. Perhaps the most glowing praise came from the esteemed science-fiction writer Ray Bradbury, who called *Close Encounters* "the most important film of our time."

After a string of successes, it seemed inevitable that Steven would one day have to face failure. That failure came with his next picture, *1941.* The 1979 film, starring comedians John Belushi and Dan Aykroyd, recounted a fictional attack on Los Angeles by the Japanese in the early days of World War II. It told of the anti-Japanese hysteria that ran rampant in the United States—especially on the West Coast, where many Japanese Americans lived—after the attack on Pearl Harbor.

The film cost $31.5 million to make, which was $5 million over budget. It was one of the most expensive films made up until that time and took an incredible 247 days to shoot. Critics pounced on the film. One called it "a movie that will live in infamy," recalling the words of Franklin D. Roosevelt after the bombing of Pearl Harbor. Its racism and lack of historical accuracy offended others. Any critic who had harbored doubts about the young director's skills used *1941* as an example of his single-minded interest in high-tech special effects, which were largely to blame for the overwhelming cost of the film. Steven told a *New York Times* reporter, "I'll spend the rest of my life disowning this movie."

Fortunately, better days were on the horizon. Back in 1977, he and George Lucas had talked about making a film together. Lucas had just finished *Star Wars,* and he and Spielberg took a quick trip to Hawaii. While building a sandcastle, Lucas asked Steven what he wanted to do next. Steven replied that he would like to make a James Bond movie. Lucas said that he had something even better, a film called *Raiders of the Lost Ark*, about an archeologist's adventurous search for the Ark of the Covenant, a powerful religious icon. Lucas declared that it would be like the old-fashioned adventure stories they had enjoyed as kids.

Once Lucas and Spielberg sold the idea to Paramount, they set to work. They hired Lawrence Kasdan to write the script, which featured the fedora-wearing archeologist-adventurer named Indiana Jones. As he always did, Steven, with the help of four artists, create storyboards that planned out each moment of the film. In 1980 the cast and crew traveled to North African to begin filming. Harrison Ford starred as Indiana Jones, and Karen Allen played the female lead, Marion Ravenwood. Steven finished the film ahead of schedule, taking just sixteen weeks to complete it. He also came in under budget, the first time he had ever done so.

Raiders of the Lost Ark was a huge hit with audiences, although critics were less enthusiastic. The movie was too violent for some people, and others disapproved of its racial stereotypes. But the public could not get enough of the movie, and *Raiders* was the box-office champion of 1981. Steven received another Oscar nomination for best director, although he again did not win. The film's success was enough to guarantee that two sequels would be made: *Indiana Jones and the Temple of Doom* (1984) and *Indiana Jones and the Last Crusade* (1989).

One remarkable thing that came out of directing *Raiders* was that it convinced Steven that he did not want to spend his career making action films. "I felt like I was losing touch with the reason I became a moviemaker—to make stories about people and relationships." Steven says he began wishing he had a friend to confide in and began to dream up an imaginary creature. "Then I thought, 'What if I were ten years old again . . . and what if he needed me as much as I needed him?" And so was born the idea for *E.T.*

Spielberg put a lot of himself and his child-hood into the heartwarming sci-fi film *E.T.* Here he works with star Henry Thomas, who played the boy who finds and befriends the gentle space traveler.

Chapter 5

An Emotional Journey

IN 1980, HARRISON Ford's girlfriend, screenwriter Melissa Mathison, visited the set of *Raiders of the Lost Ark*. She and Steven began to talk about his new idea, the story of a lonely boy from a divorced family and his alien friend. Mathison was interested in the story, and they agreed that the creature should be loving and gentle. Steven asked Mathison to write the script, and she set to work in October 1980. She was not interested in the science-fiction part of the story, but rather in "the idea of an alien creature who was benevolent, tender, emotional, and sweet. . . . The idea of the creature's striking up a relationship with a child who came from a broken home was very affecting."

Steven has said that *E.T.* is "a very personal story . . . about the divorce of my parents, how I felt when my parents broke up." Perhaps the film's honest and genuine emotion is one reason why it had the power to touch so many people. Eleven-year-old Henry Thomas plays Elliot, the lonely boy who finds the stranded alien and declares, "I'm keeping him!" Elliot's father is absent from the story, and his mother is so distracted and upset by her divorce that she fails to notice for some time that an alien is living in her house. For Elliot, *E.T.* becomes a father figure and friend. Likewise, Elliot finds joy in caring for the homesick creature, and E.T.'s presence brings him closer to his brother and sister—and eventually to his mother.

Near the end of the film, E.T. manages to contact his own family so he can go home. As much as Elliot wants him to stay, he knows that E.T. is homesick. As the spaceship is ready to depart, E.T. says, "Come." Elliot replies, "Stay." Yet they both know that either choice is impossible. Elliot and E.T. must stay with their families.

Two other young people, Robert MacNaughton and six-year-old Drew Barrymore, played Elliot's brother and sister. For the first time in his career, Steven decided not to use storyboards, in part because he was working with young people. "I decided that storyboards might smother the spontaneous reaction that young children might have to a sequence," he said. "So I purposely didn't do any story-boards and just came onto the set and winged it every day and made the movie as close to my own sensibilities and instincts as I possibly could." Steven's idea was right on the mark, for he produced a genuine, touching story about the difficulties of a broken family and the importance of friendship. Not using storyboards allowed him to be more flexible and to concentrate on the emotional aspects of the film, rather than on the technical aspects.

Steven took special care in working with the children to draw out the best performances possible. He treated them as equals and felt that the best way to work with Henry Thomas was "not to be his director but his buddy." In fact, the two spent their lunchtimes playing video games together. Steven always took the time to talk to the children before filming the most difficult scenes. Drew Barrymore has said that in scenes in which the actors had to cry, Steven always spent time helping them to feel the emotion. "He had this special way of talking to you, and his voice would change and it made you cry. There was something so gentle about it," she recalled in an interview, eighteen years after making the film. According to biographer Joseph McBride, just before filming the scene in which *E.T.* is dying, Steven spoke quietly to Henry Thomas. "It'll be sadder if it's happy-sad," he said. "I think *you'll* feel sadder if it's more you're trying to cover that up, trying to cover the sadness with some happy talk to E.T."

The emotional side of *E.T.* is what made it such a huge hit, but Steven's eye for the technical aspects of moviemaking was still an important part of the film. He knew that E.T. had to look not only lovable, but realistic as well, and that this would be no small feat. He called on Carlo Rambaldi, the Italian artist who had created Puck for *Close Encounters,* to take on the job. At first, Rambaldi planned to make a single live-action puppet, but he realized that he actually need two creatures, one that could walk by itself and another for close-ups of E.T.'s remarkably expressive face. In addition, certain scenes were shot with small actors dressed as E.T. Although Steven has described E.T. as "a creature that only a mother could love," he enchanted audiences all over the world. Two of his most remarkable features were his glowing heart and the long fingertip that lit up, both to express love and to heal. Henry Thomas recalled the effect the creature had on him. In the final scene of the film, when his character must say good-bye to E.T., Thomas "couldn't stop crying because I worked with E.T. every day and he was very real to me."

The choice of cameraman was another vital aspect in the making of *E.T.* Out of the blue, Steven called up his old friend Allen Daviau, who had been the cinematographer for *Amblin'* so many years before. He said, "How would you like to photograph my next feature?" Daviau was stunned. He had worked only on television movies up to that time. Now Hollywood's most famous director was calling to offer him a job!

As Daviau learned more about the project, he knew that the cinematography would be an important part of the film. "It's got to be so real," he said, "so that the magic that happens isn't hokey." Lighting became an important part of the filmmaking process. To make E.T. look more realistic, Daviau and Steven kept the light on the creature soft and muted, so that he could just barely be seen, especially in the early scenes of the film. Daviau recalled that if there was just a bit too much light on Rambaldi's creature, the effect was disastrous—E.T. looked like a plastic and rubber puppet, not a living creature. If there was not enough light, he simply could not be seen. It was Daviau's excellent skills with light that ultimately made E.T. seem so real. "E.T. could not only look sad, but he could look curiously sad," remarked Steven, "not by the way we controlled E.T. mechanically but by the way Allen shifted light."

Steven demanded a lot of his cinematographer, and at

A six-year-old Drew Barrymore captured audiences' hearts with her portrayal of Elliot's sister in *E.T.* Spielberg abandoned his traditional storyboards when working with the kids and decided instead to let the children's own improvisations guide each day's filming.

times the work was frustrating. But, ultimately, the Spielberg demand for perfection pushed Daviau to achieve remarkable things. Once John Williams's music was added to the mix, *E.T.* was ready to go.

In May 1982, the movie premiered at the famous Cannes Film Festival in France. The audience was thrilled. Near the film's end, when E.T.'s finger lights up to show that he is alive, people began to light matches. It was as if the theater were filled with stars. People clapped, yelled, and stomped their feet in appreciation of the film. A searchlight swept to the balcony, where a smiling Steven looked on at the spectacle. Soon people around the world would share the remarkable feeling the movie had inspired in this audience.

In June, Steven was invited to show *E.T.* to President and Mrs. Ronald Reagan at the White House. "Nancy Reagan was crying toward the end," Steven recalled, "and the President looked like a ten-year-old kid." Steven then showed the film at the United Nations and was awarded the UN Peace Medal to honor the its message. Steven even met Queen Elizabeth when *E.T.* was presented at a royal benefit. Eventually, *E.T.* became the top-grossing film of all time (in the United States), surpassing even *Star Wars*. It held the number-one spot until 1997, when *Star Wars* was released again and recaptured the lead. The following year, *Titanic* took over the lead, a record it continued to hold into 2002.

Most critics raved about *E.T.* Roger Ebert said, "This is not simply a good movie. It is one of the rare movies that brush[es] away our cautions and win our hearts." Another proclaimed that Spielberg had "for the first time, put his breathtaking technical skills at the service of his deepest feelings." The movie was nominated for nine Academy Awards, including best director. This time the award went to Richard Attenborough, who directed *Gandhi*. When Attenborough's name was called, he did not go immediately to the podium to accept his award but went first to where Steven sat. He embraced Steven and said, "This isn't right, this should be yours" and then went to receive his award. Attenborough later said that he considered *E.T.* the "more exciting, wonderful, innovative piece of film." (Years later, Attenborough would star in Steven's film *Jurassic Park.*)

Steven appreciated Attenborough's kindness, even calling it "an honorary Oscar." But it was painful to have been overlooked once again by the Academy. "I've been around long enough to know that people who deserve Oscars don't always win them."

Whether or not the Academy recognized his achievement, *E.T.* stayed in theaters for one full year before the studio decided to remove it. (The plan was to release it again in two years, hoping that absence would make audiences' hearts grow fonder.) During that year, two hundred million people around the world saw *E.T.* As of 2002, it was still the fourth top-grossing film of all time in the United States. The film was re-released in 2002 in honor of its twentieth anniversary. Steven Spielberg's beloved extraterrestrial would touch a whole new generation.

After *E.T.,* Steven worked one segment of *Twilight Zone— The Movie,* a trilogy directed by three different filmmakers, each based on the popular 1950s television show. He was also one of the film's producers. The project turned into a nightmare when a deadly accident took place on the set of another director's segment. Tragically, actor Vic Morrow and two young children were killed. The bad press and ill will that surrounded the project turned the *The Twilight Zone—The Movie* into a disaster. When it opened in 1983 it received mixed reviews and only limited box-office success.

Next, Steven teamed up once again with George Lucas to make the first sequel to *Raiders of the Lost Ark, Indiana Jones and the Temple of Doom,* released in 1984. After the child-friendly *E.T.* and the huge acclaim it garnered, *The Temple of Doom* came as something of a surprise to Spielberg fans. The movie was much more violent than the first Indiana Jones feature, and Lucas and Steven were criticized. At first, Steven justified the film, saying that the violent images were all imaginary, things that could never happen in real life. But later he admitted that the movie was "too dark . . . much too horrific" and that it would "not go down in my pantheon as one of my prouder moments." In addition to concerns over the film's violence, movie critics began to question whether Steven Spielberg would ever "grow up" and tackle films with more serious, mature themes.

1984 may not have been Steven's best year as a film-maker, but it did bring positive news. First, his girlfriend, actress Amy Irving, became pregnant, and Steven was thrilled. While working with the child actors on *E.T.,* Steven had said that he almost felt like their father, and afterward, he described having "a deep yearning" to become a parent. In addition, Steven and two producers, Kathleen Kennedy and Frank Marshall, formed Amblin Entertainment. Running his own filmmaking company would give Steven the opportunity to help other young filmmakers make their projects happen. It also meant that he could do more of the films that truly interested him. One of these was *The Color Purple.*

In 1983, Steven's partner Kathleen Kennedy brought him author Alice Walker's book *The Color Purple* saying that she thought he would enjoy it. The book, which won the Pulitzer Prize, takes place in the South during the first part of the twentieth century. It tells the story of an African American woman named Celie who is abused first by her father and then by her husband, a man she calls not by his first name, but simply "Mr."

Walker writes from a strong feminist perspective, contending that while all African Americans faced severe racism, African American women struggled because of their gender as well. No matter how difficult life could be for a black man in the South, it would always be tougher for a woman. But through all of the painful events in her life, the character of Celie perseveres and endures, ultimately to find happiness.

Over the years, Steven had told Kennedy about some of his childhood experiences with prejudice. She believed that, because he was Jewish, he might have a special understanding of Walker's message—perhaps it would strike a chord in him. As Kennedy had predicted, Steven loved the book. He came away admiring Celie and wanting to make a movie about her. He agreed to take on the project as a producer, working with coproducers Kennedy and Frank Marshall, as well as with the respected composer Quincy Jones. But at first he was not sure that he wanted to direct it. The idea excited him, but it also scared him. He confided in Jones, asking if a black director or a woman might be a better choice for the project. Jones relied, "You didn't have to come from Mars to do *E.T.,* did you?" Steven was convinced. It was time for him to move in another, more serious, direction as a filmmaker.

The next step was meeting Alice Walker, who needed to be sure that the film would be true to her novel. Walker was not certain that she wanted the movie made, because Hollywood had so often depicted African Americans as stereotypes. "I had never seen a film that had black people in real character roles, you know, where they were actually real people. They were only servants and maids and stereotypes," she has said.

Steven later joked that meeting with Walker was like a job interview—and he had not gone on a job interview for eleven years. Still, she agreed to sit down with Steven and immediately recognized that he had read the book very carefully and that he understood the spirit of her work. She decided

Adapting Alice Walker's book *The Color Purple* to the screen posed new challenges for Spielberg. Many, including Spielberg himself, were not convinced that a white director could do justice to this story of African Americans. Although the film received 11 Oscar nominations, it captured no awards.

to trust him with the project. "When Steven Spielberg appeared, there was a part of me that saw it as a magical thing. . . . There was something about this person appearing, open-hearted, very intense and very loving toward this book," she said.

Others did not know if he was the right director for the job. Almost immediately, people began asking why a white male director, especially Steven Spielberg, was making

The Color Purple. Some claimed his sole motivation was to win the illusive Academy Award that he had been thus far denied. These rumors must have disturbed him, but Steven admitted that he was ready to make a change in his career—and ready for audiences to expect something different from him. "I really wanted to challenge myself with something that was not stereotypically a Spielberg movie. Not to try to prove anything, or to show off—but just to try to use a different set of muscles," he told an interviewer in 1985. In *The Color Purple,* he reflected, "the characters are the story."

Alice Walker played an important role in the production. She helped to make casting decisions, including the choice of comedian Whoopi Goldberg to play the role of Celie. Goldberg had asked Walker to consider her for the smaller role of Sofia, a part that later went to talk-show host Oprah Winfrey. When Walker saw Goldberg perform her one-woman comedy show, she recommended that Steven cast her as Celie. *The Color Purple* would be Goldberg's first film, and she was widely praised for her work. As for Oprah Winfrey, she had never acted before, but Steven remembered that she "convinced me that she *was* this character in our first meeting. . . . I cast her and she was wonderful."

In addition to playing a role in casting the film, Walker also submitted a screenplay to the producers, but it was ultimately rejected. The novel contains many difficult subjects, which were echoed in her screenplay. Steven and the other producers opted to use a script that would be less controversial. Nonetheless, Walker was often available on the set to add lines to the script and to help the cast with the dialogue. This way, she could ensure that their speech was consistent with that of the period in which the story took place. Walker also had the opportunity to make sure that she agreed with the way *The Color Purple* was portrayed on film, even if it differed from her book.

Filming began in June 1985. For the second time in his career, Steven chose not to use storyboards. "The first time was *E.T.,* because it was an emotional journey. I felt that *The Color Purple* was even more of an emotional journey, and I wanted to surprise myself through the process of discovery every day during the making of the movie. I was afraid the storyboards would tie me down to preconceived ideas that would no longer be relevant once the cast got together."

Although much of the picture would be filmed on location in North Carolina, the cast and crew stayed in Los Angeles for the first week, in part because Amy Irving was due to give birth at any time. As they were filming the scene in which Celie gives birth, Steven received a phone call. It was Irving, informing him that she was in labor. Max Samuel Spielberg was born on June 13, 1985, which Steven said was his "best production of the year." He recorded Max crying at home, and when Celie's baby cries in *The Color Purple,* it is actually Max the audience hears. Five months later, Steven and Amy were married.

The Color Purple opened in theaters on December 18, 1985, and did very well at the box office. Although it had cost just $15 million to make, it earned $142.7 million worldwide. Many critics put it on their "top-ten" lists for the year, and most gave it good reviews. But some critics were vicious in their attacks on *The Color Purple.* One said that Steven "finds it harder to imagine black people than spacemen." Others accused him of offering a racist view of black men as abusive monsters, refusing to acknowledge that the movie was based on the work of an African American author.

The Color Purple received eleven Academy Award nominations, including ones for best picture and best actress (Whoopi Goldberg), two for best supporting actress (Oprah Winfrey and Margaret Avery), and one for best cinematographer (Allen Daviau). But with all of this recognition, the director was ignored. Steven Spielberg was not nominated as best director for *The Color Purple,* and many believed that this omission was a tremendous insult—and a petty snub. Perhaps even worse, the film did not win a single Oscar. Steven did receive the Directors Guild of America Award that year, a great honor. If he was disappointed about the Oscar, he tried not to let it show. "Certainly, anybody would feel hurt to be left out of a category of richly deserved nominations, but I'm not bitter or angry about it," he said. Later, he did admit that he believed that the Academy was punishing him for his box-office success, refusing to give him credit for a job well done.

After this painful experience, some people expected Steven to go back to the kind of moviemaking that was expected of him. They predicted that his next project would be another science-fiction fantasy or an action-packed Indiana Jones flick. It may have come as a surprise, then, that he was determined to make another serious film.

Empire of the Sun is set in China during World War II, a period that would resonate throughout Steven's work in the years ahead. Like *E.T.,* the film features a child actor, but instead of a young man who has a spiritual encounter with a benevolent alien, young Jim Graham, the main character of *Empire of the Sun,* lives in a horrific world of hunger, disease, and misery.

At the beginning of the film, Jim, played by Christian

Bale, is a rich British schoolboy living in Shanghai at the dawn of World War II. He becomes separated from his parents when a mob of Chinese refugees struggles to flee the invading Japanese army. Alone, he is sent to a Japanese prison camp. Jim is eleven at the start of the film. As he struggles to survive and to understand the loss of both his parents and his way of life, the harsh reality of his new circumstances forces him to grown up. Steven saw a connection between Jim's own loss of innocence and the changes that took place in the world after World War II. "I wanted to draw a parallel story between the death of this boy's innocence and the death of innocence of the entire world."

Empire of the Sun opened to mixed reviews—and to little interest at the box office. Steven joked that he had earned the right to fail commercially. "I knew going in that *Empire of the Sun* wasn't a very commercial project, it wasn't going to have a broad audience appeal," he told one interviewer. "But it was a story about a courageous survivor who was only 13 years old. And I so identified with him in the novel. I knew I had to make this movie. . . . Some things need to be done regardless of the commercial return."

One critic wrote that he hoped that "Steven Spielberg's *Empire of the Sun* wins him that damn Oscar so he goes back to making movies that give real and lasting pleasure." It seemed that no matter what Steven did, whether a film was youthful or mature, silly or serious, someone would have something negative to say. Likewise, the Academy snubbed him yet one more time, giving the film six nominations, but no recognition for his direction. Cinematographer Allen Daviau, with whom Steven had collaborated once again, was nominated for his camera work. "I feel very sorry that I get nominations and Steven doesn't," he said. "It's his vision that makes it all come together."

In *Empire of the Sun,* Spielberg returned to his interest in World War II. The film centers on the experiences of a British school-boy living in China when the Japanese invade.

After two emotionally draining films, Steven was ready for something different. He had promised George Lucas that he would direct one more Indiana Jones film. Promise or no promise, Steven said, "The real reason I'm doing *Indy III* is because I want to have fun." Although it would prove to be an easier project than the previous two, it was time-consuming. Steven wanted the last of the Indiana Jones films to act as an exciting finale to the trilogy. It took four tries to get the screenplay right. Steven wished to make a father and son story, but Lucas wanted the movie to be about the quest for the Holy Grail. Finally, *The Last Crusade* became not only a quest for the Holy Grail, but also Indy's quest for his father.

At about this time, Steven was experiencing major changes in his personal life. The stress of two film careers in one family had taken a toll on his marriage to actress Amy Irving. In 1989 the couple divorced. Steven became involved with actress Kate Capshaw, who had starred in *The Temple of Doom.* Like Steven, Kate had a child from a previous marriage. She also had a foster child, a young boy named Theo, whom she and Steven later adopted. In 1990, Kate and Steven had their first child, a daughter named Sasha. Kate converted to Judaism, and the couple married.

The Last Crusade became Steven's most successful film since *E.T.,* earning nearly $495 million worldwide. It received respectful reviews, and many audiences were pleased to have "the old Spielberg" back behind the camera. Likewise, his next two movies, *Always* and *Hook,* did not challenge him to grow as a filmmaker. *Hook* is a modern-day version of Peter Pan. *Always* tells the story of a pilot who is killed in a plane crash but returns to Earth for the woman he loves. After taking a beating from critics for his attempts at making mature films, Steven seemed to have set aside his interest in pleasing them or winning an Academy Award—but not for long.

Back in 1982, Universal had bought the film rights to Thomas Keneally's book about the Holocaust, *Schindler's List.* Universal's Sid Sheinberg believed that the subject would be a challenging one for Steven—both as a film-maker and as a person. Steven agreed to make the picture, but he worried about it for the next decade. In 1989 an interviewer asked Steven if he was going to make *Schindler's List.* He replied that Amblin Entertainment would produce the film with Universal. "But at the moment, I'm not directing it. It's been a burdensome subject. It's a subject that's dangerous."

Steven struggled in the years that followed, debating what he should do about *Schindler's List.* It became evident that he had to make the film. Events in his personal life played a role in his decision. After Capshaw converted to Judaism, their family began to view their beliefs and religious practices more intensely. Having children made him think more seriously about the importance of honoring his background. Steven also wanted to face his own painful feelings about his experience with anti-Semitism as a boy.

World events also strengthened Steven's resolve. News stories told of "ethnic cleansing" in Bosnia, where Muslims were being murdered for their beliefs just as the Jews had been during World War II. "On top of all that comes the media giving serious air time and print space to Holocaust deniers," Steven recalled, "the people who claim that the Holocaust never happened, that six million weren't killed, that it's all some hoax." Steven wanted to ensure that the Holocaust would not be forgotten.

It was time to tell the true story of Oskar Schindler—and of the Holocaust. Doing so would change Steven Spielberg's career—and his life—forever.

Perhaps Spielberg's greatest challenge was creating the Holocaust film *Schindler's List*. The film tells the story of Oskar Schindler (seen here)— a German factory owner who saved more than 1,100 Jews from the gas chamber by hiring them in his factory. Spielberg handled this delicate subject with grace, and at last earned the Oscar for Best Director.

Chapter 6

A Turning Point

OSKAR SCHINDLER SAVED more than eleven hundred Jews during the Holocaust, but his story is not a simple one, for he was a member of the Nazi Party. Schindler hired Jews to labor in his metalworking factory, where they made supplies for the German army. In so doing, he earned a fortune. His motives for hiring Jewish labor were selfish at first; it saved him money. But as he witnessed the atrocities committed against the Jews, especially the liquidation of the Jewish ghetto in Krakow, Poland, he reached a turning point. He used the fortune he had amassed to save the lives of the

Jews who worked for him. "What would drive a man like this to suddenly take everything he had earned and put it all in the service of saving these lives?" Steven wondered.

As he thought about how he would make *Schindler's List*, Steven knew it would have to be long movie to do the story justice. He considered filming it in black and white so it would be more like a documentary or the newsreels that were shown in theaters during World War II. He believed that color could not tell the story of the Holocaust as he envisioned it. "I knew the minute I read the book that I would be making this film someday in black and white." It would be difficult to convince the studio to let him make a three-hour, black-and-white film about one of the most horrific events in history. "I guaranteed the studio they'd lose all their money," Steven recalled. "That's how pessimistic I was that there was a climate ready to accept . . . a movie about racial hatred. I was happily wrong."

Steven offered to forego any salary to make the film. His own reputation in Hollywood and Universal's faith in him may be the only reasons that he was able to make the film the way he wanted to. "Nobody else could have gotten any studio to say yes to this project," Steven said. He knew that it was his enormous success as a filmmaker that gave him the power to make a movie he felt so strongly about. Universal executives said that he could make *Schindler's List* on one condition: that he make *Jurassic Park* first.

In 1989 author Michael Crichton gave Steven his latest book to read. It was a novel about dinosaurs called *Jurassic Park*. Steven knew immediately that Crichton's tale would make a great movie. It was the story of a billionaire (played by Richard Attenborough) who finds a way to clone dinosaurs after discovering DNA preserved in amber. He comes up with a plan to open a theme park with live dinosaurs. "Our attraction will drive kids out of their minds," proclaims Attenborough's character. What he did not predict was that the animals would run amuck, destroying both him and the park, and nearly killing his young grandchildren as well.

Steven wanted to buy the film rights for *Jurassic Park*, but so did almost every studio in Hollywood. Finally, Crichton chose Steven to produce and direct the film. He knew that it would be a difficult story to bring to the screen and that it would require an innovative film-maker to make it happen. "Steven is arguably the most experienced and most successful director of these kinds of movies."

Soon after, Steven met with Crichton to discuss the characters in the book. As the two continued to talk, Crichton asked Steven how he intended to create the dinosaurs for the film. Steven shrugged and said that that was not important. "Effects are only as good as the audience's feeling for the characters," he said. In truth, Steven himself was not sure at the time how it would be done.

Pre-production of *Jurassic Park* began in June 1990. Preparations were so complicated that it would take almost two years before filming could begin. As he so often did, Steven worked with artists to make storyboards of the scenes. He used them to plan the action and special effects. Once filming began, the storyboards for a given scene were always on the set on the day that it was to be shot. Steven would review them carefully with the cast and crew before the cameras rolled.

Designer Stan Winston was hired to build intricate

life-sized models of the dinosaurs. Steven also had miniature models made for scenes showing dinosaurs stampeding. But once the miniatures were complete, he did not think that they looked realistic. He decided to talk to the special-effects wizards at Industrial Light and Magic (ILM), a company owned by George Lucas. When Steven was told that the artists at ILM could create full-sized dinosaurs with computer graphics, Steven was not convinced. "I thought it was possible that *someday* they might be able to create three-dimensional, live-action characters through computer graphics. But I didn't think it would happen this soon." Steven told the ILM artists to prove it. And prove it they did.

When he saw the first computer-generated images of the dinosaurs, Steven knew he was watching the future of filmmaking unfold before his eyes. He had never seen anything look so authentic. Together with the life-sized models, the computer graphics would help him to make the most realistic movie ever about dinosaurs. The prehistoric creatures of *Jurassic Park* were about to become movie stars. After opening in the summer of 1993, the film became a blockbuster hit, earning $913 million worldwide.

Earlier that year, after the filming of *Jurassic Park* had been completed, Steven left for Poland, where he would begin work on *Schindler's List*, the most difficult experience of his career. Recreating the Holocaust was overwhelming, and Steven described himself as "constantly sickened" and "frightened every day" during filming. He says that, while making the movie, he was "hit in the face with my personal life. My upbringing. My Jewishness. The stories my grand-parents told me about the Shoah. . . . I cried all the time." (*Shoah* is the Hebrew word for Holocaust.)

Before Spielberg could make *Schindler's List,* the studio required that he make *Jurassic Park,* an effects-driven adventure about revived dinosaurs run wild on an island theme park. A king-size hit, *Jurassic Park* has spawned a wave of interest in dinosaurs and two sequels.

Although there was still work to be done on *Jurassic Park, Schindler's List* had to be filmed during the wintertime. George Lucas took over some of the postproduction tasks for *Jurassic Park,* but Steven still wanted to keep control of the movie's soundtrack and any last-minute decisions about the computer-generated dinosaurs. He set up a high-tech communication system that allowed him to see the images that the ILM artists created and to hear the music that John Williams wrote. Each night, when he had finished shooting scenes for *Schindler's List,* he went back to his hotel to work on *Jurassic Park.* Although it was difficult to go back and forth between movies with such very different themes, the break that *Jurassic Park* gave him from the difficult subject matter of *Schindler's List* may have helped him to work through the horrors of recreating the Holocaust. The presence of his family was also a comfort to him during this time. Kate and their five children had accompanied him to Poland, and the family lived together in a small hotel. Steven's parents and rabbi also came to visit from time to time.

Making *Schindler's List* was also a difficult technical feat. The massive production involved 126 speaking parts. There were three thousand extras, many of whom did not speak English. Translators were hired to tell them, in several different languages, what Steven wanted them to do. There were 148 sets shot at 35 different locations. The actors and extras often had to be up and ready to do their scenes by 5 A.M., often in bitterly cold weather. But, through the three months of production, Steven, his cast, and his crew were dedicated to making the best possible film. Shooting at actual locations where the story took place, including the ghetto streets in Krakow, Schindler's factory, and Krakow's Nazi headquarters and prison, made the process profoundly emotional. Steven said, "I was standing where, as a Jew, I couldn't have stood fifty years before."

John Williams was called upon to compose the score for *Schindler's List.* When Steven showed him the completed film, he was deeply moved—so much so that he was not sure that he was up to the task of composing its score. "You need a better composer than I am," he said to Steven. "I know, but they're all dead," Steven replied. In the end, Williams wrote one of the most moving works of his great career. When Steven heard the music, he suggested using a violin for the theme. Williams called world-famous Israeli violinist Itzhak Pearlman, who agreed to perform the music for the soundtrack. The result was a haunting and poignant complement to the film.

In December 1993, when *Schindler's List* opened in theaters, critics hailed the work as a masterpiece. Terrence Rafferty of the *New Yorker* called it "the finest, fullest dramatic (that is, nondocumentary) film ever made about the Holocaust." Another wrote, "Mr. Spielberg has made sure that neither he nor the Holocaust will ever be thought of in the same way again. . . . It's as if he understood for the first time why God gave him such extraordinary skills." In making this profound work of art, Steven Spielberg had proven himself once and for all. For the second time, he won the Directors Guild of America Award. In March 1994, at long last, he won the Oscar for best director. *Schindler's List* won six other Academy Awards that year, including one for best picture. It was also a box-office success, earning $321.2 million worldwide.

When asked what movie he would make next, Steven said, "I have no idea what to do next. And, more important, I don't care." After *Schindler's List,* Steven waited three years before starting to work on another film. During that time, he founded the Survivors of the Shoah Visual History Foundation, funded with $6 million of his own money— money earned from *Schindler's List.* In fact, Steven donated all of his earnings from the film to Jewish organizations and historical projects, such as the U.S. Holocaust Museum in Washington, D.C.

Steven founded the Survivors of the Shoah in 1994. Its purpose is to record the testimonies of Holocaust survivors. He says that after *Schindler's List,* many Holocaust survivors came to him saying, "I have a story to tell. Will you hear my story?" At first he thought they were asking him to make a movie of their stories. "But," Steven recalls, "what they were really saying was, 'Will you take my testimony? Can I, before I die, tell some-body—tell you, with a camera—what happened to me, so my children will know, so my friends will finally know, and so I can leave something of myself behind so the world will know?'"

Making *Schindler's List* had brought about tremendous change in Steven's life. He realized the importance of his religion, of his people. He wanted to educate young people about the Holocaust and to make sure that the stories of the survivors would be heard. Today, the Survivors of the Shoah has developed an audiovisual archive of survivors' taped accounts. Volunteer interviewers (many survivors themselves) and camera crews have conducted interviews all over the world, in 57 countries and in 32 languages. At the start of the project, there were an estimated 300,000 living survivors. "We set a goal of interviewing 50,000 survivors," Steven says. "This was such a crusade, and so many people volun-teered their time. I wanted to disseminate information told by the survivors to middle and high school children all over the U.S. and Europe. We have now taped 51,000 'educators,' survivors who reach out through CD-ROM or video to teach young people about the crime of the century. I hear children who watch it say,

The story of Oskar Schindler was not an easy one to direct. Spielberg chose to tell the story anyway, shooting the film in black and white to give it a documentary feeling. In 1994, Spielberg founded the Survivors of Shoah to record the testimonies of Holocaust survivors and to ensure that the world does not forget the sacrifice of those who died.

'I didn't know this happened.' The naïveté is shocking."

Another important event in Steven's life in 1994 was the founding of DreamWorks SKG, the production company that Steven started with friends Jeffrey Katzenberg, former chairman of Disney Studios, and David Geffen, founder of Geffen records. The press called this partnership of highly successful Hollywood leaders "The Dream Team." Steven suggested that they make the name "DreamWorks" and add the initials of their last names to it: DreamWorks SKG.

The company produces films, television programs, music, and interactive videos. Its goal is to give young artists a chance to create their own work, as well as to guarantee the partners full control over their projects. In addition to producing creative projects, DreamWorks also takes charge of distributing them. At forty-eight years old, Steven felt ready to take on the responsibility of running such an ambitious company with his partners.

As for making films, Steven had not lost touch with the more magical and light-hearted side of moviemaking. When he returned to filmmaking in 1997, he announced that he planned to go back and forth from "entertainment to socially conscious movies." And, to date, he has proven his ability to do just that. The first film he chose to work on after *Schindler's List* was *The Lost World,* a sequel to *Jurassic Park,* which was released in 1997. Later that year, one of DreamWorks' first films, *Amistad,* was released. Directed by Steven, *Amistad* is based on the true story of a group of African captives who took over a ship that was transporting them to a life of slavery. The film received good reviews, although it did not do well at the box office.

Steven's next film, his last of the twentieth century, was *Saving Private Ryan.* Steven had been interested in World War II since childhood, in part because of his father's stories of wartime experiences, and he had already tackled the subject of World War II, both as a young amateur filmmaker and as a professional

Hollywood director. The Indiana Jones films were set in the World War II era. *1941, Empire of the Sun,* and *Schindler's List* each depict the war from a different perspective. But, to date, Steven had not made a film about combat—at least not since his teenage war movies, *Fighter Squad* and *Escape to Nowhere.* In 1998 he was ready to explore the horrific reality of war. "For years now, I've been looking for the right World War II story to shoot," he said, "and when Robert Rodat wrote *Saving Private Ryan,* I found it."

The film tells the story of an eight-man mission to find a single soldier, Private James Ryan, after the D-Day invasion at Normandy, France. Private Ryan's three brothers were all killed in action, and their mother learns the news in a single day. When a general in Washington, D.C., hears the story, he issues an order to bring Private Ryan home.

Steven did a great deal of research to ensure that the film honored the memory of those who had fought in World War II—and that it would remind people of their sacrifice. "The last thing we wanted to do in this picture," he says, "was use the war simply as a springboard for action-adventure. I was looking for realism all the time." Steven talked to veterans of the war, men who had actually landed at Omaha Beach in Normandy on D-Day—June 6, 1944. He listened to their stories as he began to think of how he would capture the experience of war on film.

In August 1997, Steven had his key actors go through boot camp before filming began. Captain Dale Dye of the U.S. Marine Corps was the military adviser for the film. He led the actors through ten physically and emotionally grueling days of basic training. Dye wanted

For years, Spielberg had sought the ideal World War II film to direct.
He found that film in *Saving Private Ryan,* the story of one troop during
the U.S. invasion of Nazi-held France in June 1944. Spielberg's efforts
earned the film four Oscars and provided a tribute to the sacrifices of
American servicemen.

the actors to know what it was like to be a soldier—and it was anything but easy. "I believe there is a certain core spirit that is common among men and women who fight for their country, and I think to understand it fully, the actors playing them need to experience the rigors that combat people all over the world face," Dye said. "So, to the extent I can, I immerse the actors in that lifestyle: I take them to the field; I make them eat rations; I make them crawl and sleep in the mud and the cold and the dirt. . . . And when they come out, if I've done my job successfully, they have an inkling of what people sacrifice to serve their country in the military."

One of the actors, Ed Burns, called boot camp the worst experience of his life. Many of the men wanted to drop out. But Tom Hanks, taking on the role of leader that he would also play in the film, pushed them to go on, reminding them how the real-life soldiers of World War II went through basic training. "We've got to do this. All the men in that squad were here." In the end, boot camp helped the actors to understand what it is like to be a soldier. "The actors arrived both willing and able to win the war," Steven said.

The movie begins, after a brief modern-day scene at Normandy, with a realistic, twenty-five minute depiction of the D-Day landing. Steven decided to shoot it on a beach in Ireland, in part because Omaha Beach is a protected landmark. He believed it inappropriate to shoot a film there. "Omaha Beach is a place to say prayers, not a place to re-create an event," he said. Veterans and historians alike have said this sequence is the most realistic portrayal of war ever put on film, and, for this reason, it is difficult to watch. Steven believed that many people would not want to see it. He told his cast not to expect *Saving Private Ryan* to be a commercially successful film, but to think of it as a memorial to World War II veterans, telling them, "We're thanking all those guys, your grandparents and my dad, who fought in World War II."

To Steven's surprise, when the film opened in July 1998, it was the number-one film in the country. Eventually, it became the most financially successful war movie ever made. Critics called it "truly remarkable" and "a soberly magnificent film." *Saving Private Ryan* was another masterpiece by the man whom *Time* magazine named "the most influential director of the 20th century." In 1999, Steven won his second Academy Award for best director. The movie won four other Oscars, including the ones for best picture and best cinematography. Steven Spielberg had directed and produced two of the most powerful and acclaimed movies of the century.

In the midst of his fourth decade in Hollywood, Steven Spielberg showed no sign of slowing down. In 2001 he released *A.I.: Artificial Intelligence,* his collaboration with Stanley Kubrick, a master filmmaker whom Steven greatly admired. Kubrick spent more than fifteen years developing the project before asking Steven to direct it. Steven did so, and also wrote the screenplay, after Kubrick's death in 1999. This science-fiction film tells the story of a robot, a young boy named David (played by 13-year-old Haley Joel Osment), who has been created to be the perfect child. He is sent to live with Henry and Monica, grieving parents of a boy who is in a coma. David wants his foster parents to love him, and—like Pinocchio—he wants to be real.

A year later, in 2002, Steven released his next film, *Minority Report,* another futuristic science-fiction film. Tom Cruise stars as a police officer in the year 2080, when technology has advanced to the point that crimes can be detected before they are committed. That same year, he began filming *Catch Me If You Can,* starring Tom Hanks and Leonardo DiCaprio, which tells the story of Frank Abagnale, the youngest man to ever be put on the FBI's most wanted list, for a string of impersonations and forgeries that took place over a period of five years, when he was between the ages of sixteen and twenty-one.

Today, five of Steven's films (*Schindler's List, E.T., Jaws, Raiders of the Lost Ark,* and *Close Encounters of the Third Kind)* are on the American Film Institute's list of the one hundred greatest films of all time. While maintaining a fast-paced schedule as a director, he continues to produce the films of other directors and to run his own production studio. He oversees the Survivors of the Shoah Foundation. And he manages to drop his children off at school every morning. "All important things get done in my life," he says. "I'm still home most nights by six and I'm still home on the weekends." Today, he and Kate Capshaw have six children. Steven is as dedicated to his family as he is to his legendary career.

Over the years, Steven never forgot the promise that he made to Chuck Silvers to help young filmmakers. With his two companies, Amblin Entertainment and Dream-Works SKG, he uses his own clout to help people with talent and creative ideas find their way in Hollywood. Says his friend director Robert Zemeckis, "Steven is the single most active mentoring director in Hollywood. He has taken responsibility for the power he's been given, which I guess you could suggest is the very definition of humility."

Steven Spielberg continues to entertain his audiences. Yet his films do more than entertain. In a world that has

Though he has won many awards for his work, Spielberg continues to help young directors and remains the most active mentoring director in Hollywood. His Dreamworks Studios has allowed talents like *American Beauty* director Sam Mendes (right) to reach new heights.

found it easy to forget the difficult lessons of the past, he has taught us about the Holocaust and World War II, about sacrifice and history. His films have instructed us about what it means to be human, about family, and about love.

"The majority of my films," Steven has said, "I have made to please people." Some critics may find fault with this approach, asserting that the best pictures are most often not the easiest to watch. But, in the end, films are made not only for the critics, to win an Academy Award, or even for the filmmaker. They are also made for the audience.

1946 On December 18, Steven Allan Spielberg is born in Cincinnati, Ohio to Arnold and Leah Spielberg

1949 The Spielbergs relocate to New Jersey in the first of several moves the family will make during Steven's childhood

1957 The Spielbergs move to Arizona; soon after, Steven begins to experiment with his father's new movie camera; makes his first real film, *The Last Train Wreck*

1958 To earn a Boy Scout merit badge, films a Western with his friends and family

1959 Begins work on *Escape to Nowhere,* a film about World War II

1961 A local television news program features Steven making *Escape to Nowhere,* giving him his first public notice as a filmmaker

1962 Completes *Escape to Nowhere*, which wins first prize in a statewide amateur film contest

1963 Finishes the script for *Firelight* and begins filming; meets his first Hollywood contact, Chuck Silvers, who works in the editorial department at Universal Pictures

1964 First feature-length film, *Firelight,* premieres to Phoenix audiences on March 24; Spielberg family moves to Saratoga, California; with the help of Chuck Silvers, gets a job as a clerical worker at Universal Pictures

1965 Graduates from Saratoga High School; enrolls at California State College at Long Beach and continues to spend as much time as possible at Universal Studios

1967 Attempts to make his first 35mm film, *Slipstream,* but runs out of money before he can complete it; meets a cameraman named Allen Daviau, who will collaborate on several of his future films

1968 Shoots *Amblin',* a twenty-six-minute silent film; Silvers is so impressed with the movie that he shows it to Sidney J. Sheinberg, vice president of production for Universal TV, who offers Steven a seven-year contract with Universal to direct television shows

1969   Directs "Eyes," a segment of the television movie *Night Gallery;* takes an eight-month leave of absence from Universal, hoping to direct a feature film

1970   Returning to Universal, directs an episode of *Marcus Welby, M.D.,* a popular television show

1971   After directing six well-received television shows, begins work on a feature-length television movie, *Duel,* in September; the film airs in November and receives rave reviews

1972   Directs two more episodes of television shows for Universal before convincing the studio to let him make *The Sugarland Express*

1974   *The Sugarland Express* opens in theaters in April; critics praise Steven, but the public finds the film too depressing; begins shooting *Jaws* on the Massachusetts island of Martha's Vineyard

1975   *Jaws* is released in theaters in June; by September it has become the most successful film in history up until that time

1976   Begins shooting *Close Encounters of the Third Kind*

1977   *Close Encounters* opens in theaters in November; the film is a critical and box-office success

1978   Is nominated for the Oscar for best director for *Close Encounters* but loses the award to Woody Allen; *Close Encounters* wins two Oscars (after receiving eight nominations), one for cinematography and one for sound-effects editing

1979   *1941* opens to terrible reviews

1980   While filming *Raiders of the Lost Ark,* tells screenwriter Melissa Mathison about his idea for a movie about a little boy who encounters an extraterrestrial; Mathison agrees to write the script for *E.T.*

1981   Steven and George Lucas's *Raiders of the Lost Ark* is the biggest box-office success of the year

1982 *E.T.* opens in June; becoming the number-one box-office hit of all time, a record it will hold until 1997; the film remains in theaters for one year and is nominated for nine Academy Awards; Universal acquires the film rights to Thomas Keneally's novel, *Schindler's List*

1983 *Twilight Zone—The Movie,* which features one segment directed by Steven, is released

1984 *Indiana Jones and the Temple of Doom* appears in theaters; Spielberg, Kathleen Kennedy, and Frank Marshall form a production company, Amblin Entertainment

1985 *The Color Purple* is released in December

1987 *Empire of the Sun* opens in theaters

1989 *Indiana Jones and the Last Crusade* and *Always* are released

1990 Begins production on *Jurassic Park*

1991 *Hook* is released

1993 Starts filming *Schindler's List* in March while completing postproduction work on *Jurassic Park,* which opens in theaters in June; within four months it breaks worldwide box-office records, earning $913 million; *Schindler's List* is released in December to excellent reviews

1994 Wins the Oscar for best director for *Schindler's List;* the film wins six additional Academy Awards, including one for best film; in September, founds the Survivors of the Shoah Visual History Foundation to record the stories of Holocaust survivors; in October he and partners Jeffrey Katzenberg and David Geffen announce the creation of their own film, television, music, and interactive video production company called DreamWorks SKG

1997 *The Lost World* appears in theaters, followed by *Amistad,* one of the first films produced by Dream-Works SKG

1998   *Saving Private Ryan* is released

1999   Wins a second Academy Award as best director for
Saving Private Ryan

2001   *A.I.: Artificial Intelligence* is released

2002   *Minority Report* with Tom Cruise opens on movie
screens; in February, begins filming *Catch Me
If You Can*

1964 *Firelight*

1968 *Amblin'*

1971 *Duel*

1974 *The Sugarland Express.*

1975 *Jaws*

1977 *Close Encounters*

1979 *1941*

1981 *Raiders of the Lost Ark*

1982 *E.T. The Extra-Terrestrial*

1983 *Twilight Zone—The Movie*

1984 *Indiana Jones and the Temple of Doom*

1985 *The Color Purple*

1987 *Empire of the Sun*

1989 *Indiana Jones and the Last Crusade*

1989 *Always*

1991 *Hook*

1993 *Schindler's List*

1997 *The Lost World: Jurassic Park*
      Amistad

1998 *Saving Private Ryan*

2001 *A.I. (Artificial Intelligence)*

2002 *Minority Report*

Ferber, Elizabeth. *Steven Spielberg.* Philadelphia: Chelsea House, 2000.

Friedman, Lester D., and Brent Notbohm. *Steven Spielberg Interviews.* Jackson: University Press of Mississippi, 2000.

Hamilton, Jake. *Special Effects.* New York: DK Publishing, 1998.

McBride, Joseph. *Steven Spielberg: A Biography.* New York: DeCapo Press, 1999.

O'Brien, Lisa. *Lights, Camera, Action! Making Movies and TV from the Inside Out.* Owl Communications, 1998.

Powers, Tom. *Steven Spielberg: Master Storyteller.* Minneapolis: Lerner Publications Company, 1997.

Rubin, Susan Goldman. *Steven Spielberg: Crazy for Movies.* New York: Harry N. Abrams, 2001.

Visit the Website of Steven Spielberg's production company, Dreamworks SKG:
[http://www.dreamworks.com]

To learn more about the Survivors of the Shoah Visual History Foundation, visit:
[http://www.shoahfoundation.org]

Visit the official *Saving Private Ryan* Website:
[http://www.rzm.com/pvt.ryan/]

View a list of the top fifty grossing films (U.S.) of all time:
[http://movieweb.com/movie/alltime.html]

Visit the official *E.T.* 20th Anniversary Website:
[http://www.et20.com]

Elizabeth Sirimarco is a writer and editor who lives in Denver, Colorado, with her husband, David, a cat named Roger, and a Rottweiler named Sebastian. She has written more than thirty-five books for young people on a range of diverse subjects, including Tiger Woods, Thomas Jefferson, AIDS, and the Yanomami.